"Tracy brings us the missing piece! For [...] something from our disciple-making ef[...] incredible background and engaging e[...] the faith with authenticity and connection. Small Batch Discipleship is a must read for any Christian who takes seriously their responsibility to make disciples."

Kadi Cole, Leadership Consultant, Executive Coach and Author of Developing Female Leaders. www.kadicole.com

"One of the greatest blessings in our spiritual walks has been the privilege of growing and learning with Jon and Tracy Sullivan. Their approach to discipleship and the methods Tracy lays out in this book are simple, reproducible, and powerful. As we follow Jesus' commandment in Matthew to 'go and make disciples,' this book is a perfect way to lead each of us as we lead others to know Jesus more."

Case & Kimberly Keenum, NFL Quarterback and spouse, Author of Playing for More: Trust Beyond What You Can See

"I'm not sure I have met anyone who is more passionate about discipleship than Tracy Sullivan. Her zeal inspires you to lock arms with a friend and travel the road with Jesus together. Small Batch Discipleship is just that. An opportunity to lock arms with a friend and walk through this experience of learning about God and His plans for your life. The stories are fun and action points practical. Grab a friend and get started."

Judy West, Pastor/Leadership Development at The Crossing Church, St. Louis, MO, and Leader of WXP/ Women's Executive Pastor Network

"Clarifying and brave. Hope-filled and strong. I love the stories and practicality of this book. The writing sounds just like Tracy, so inviting. Her wisdom, vision, and experience shines through. May the Spirit, through Small Batch Discipleship, sweep lives into extraordinary worship by living the Great Commission lifestyle."

Ron Surgeon, Pastor of Training, Renewal Church, Memphis, TN, and Licensed Professional Counselor, Certified Clinical Trauma Professional

"This book punched me in the gut. It opened my eyes to how simple it is to share Jesus, and how important this call is on each of our lives. Small Batch Discipleship equips and inspires anyone ready to jump into a practical and purposeful life after Christ."

Vera Schmitz, Co-founder, Dwell dwelldifferently.com

"Awakened my soul! Small Batch Discipleship has forever altered the way I look at life and how investing in people can create lasting change. In all my years as a leader and advisor to others, there has never been a better time to invest in people, and Tracy Sullivan provides a thought-provoking, God-centered, and simple framework to follow. Her ability to share God's wisdom and personal stories invites me to experience life with greater purpose. If you are looking for inspiring words, practical application and a framework to increase your impact, look no further. Change one, change the world!"

Bill Fretwell, Principal, Edward Jones

"Becoming a leader is one thing. Becoming an effective leader where it really matters is another entirely. In Small Batch Discipleship, Tracy Sullivan lovingly lays out how we can lead for effect where it matters most. And she makes a clear and compelling case for why we should all start doing so—starting today. You'll read this book in one sitting because it speaks directly to your heart. And then you'll come back to it again and again to help you grow as the leader you've been called to be."

Robert Teschner, Founder and CEO, VMax Group, and Author of Debrief to Win

"As a disciple-maker, I found Tracy's book an inspiring encouragement to continue. Many a young disciple should read this book. Tracy has clearly articulated what The Master meant to go and make disciples. It is easy to understand from the truths and examples shared what we must do to obey one of Christ's clear and final commands. Finally, an answer to the biggest question we must ask ourselves as Christians: Is your life an example of the Great Commission or the Great Omission."

Koos Basson, Director, IMD Africa

"The Sullivan family's discipleship has had a profound impact on my walk with the Lord, so it brings me great joy that Tracy has created this tool to equip others to do the same. Tracy lays out a roadmap for discipleship that is both soundly rooted in scripture and genuinely reflective of her lifestyle. Tracy provides a wealth of wisdom that will certainly point you to Jesus and challenge you to walk in obedience to His calling to 'make disciples of all nations'."

Barrett Jones, ESPN College Football Analyst, and former NFL Player

"This book will assist all women in the church to understand what Christ expected when He commanded the Church to make disciples, to produce people who love and obey God, bear fruit, and live with joy. The crisis at the heart of the church is that we often speak about making disciples, but we seldom put much effort behind doing it. So, for all women in the church ready to put words into practice, Small Batch Discipleship offers the inspiration and practical know-how to do so.

The greatest strength of this book for me is my Sister Tracy Sullivan's unrelenting emphasis that 'You've been chosen to multiply the life of Christ into small batch groups of individuals who will one day become ready, able, and willing to reproduce the same into others.' (See 2 Tim. 2:2.). This provides a firm foundation instrumental in equipping women through forming and leading small batches to finally impact the world globally. This book is a must read, moreover a manual to follow, as we start our own small batch disciples!"

Ramsy Shika, Pastor at The Word Ministry Church, Mokopane, South Africa

embrace your *greater purpose*
through handcrafted relationships

small
batch
discipleship

tracy sullivan

D.C. PRESS

For information contact : https://tracysullivan.com/small-batch

Amazon Print ISBN: 978-1-7346749-0-3

Other Formats Digital ISBN: 978-1-7346749-1-0

Other Formats Print ISBN: 978-1-7346749-2-7

D.C. Press Publishing

First Edition: August 2020

10 9 8 7 6 5 4 3 2 1

Table of Contents

Dedicated to Matthew, Tyler and Callie - my smallest batch. All my love.

How to Use
this book

What do I need to do to convince these women they could be leaders?

The majority of my professional life has been spent developing leaders. Over the years, I've encountered numerous male leaders who've sought to know how they can inspire women to see their own potential in the same way others see it. I'm catching wind of this same conversation happening inside the church. They want to invite more women to the table to share their voices, to shape the stories being written, to benefit personally in all the ways they have as leaders, and for this inspiration to be multiplied. Today, many courageous women are taking steps into unknown spaces to fulfill their true potential. They're seeking wisdom about how to make the greatest impact on the world around them, and particularly, how to make an impact for Jesus Christ.

When my husband and I were young Jesus-followers, we were discipled by a man who gave most of his eighty-plus years of life in spiritual service to others. Motivated to see them fulfill their greatest calling as disciples and disciple-makers of Christ, he authored countless books and studies on the topic and spent decades investing time into pastors and lay leaders around the world, most of them men. In one of my last conversations with him before he went to be with the Lord, I shared I had written a children's book about following Jesus, not yet in print. He read it and said it was wonderful, and that he hoped God would richly bless it along with "focused materials for women." I hadn't mentioned writing anything for women yet, but I took that as a call to do so.

This is that book. This material is for all women who believe there's something more to the Christian life than what they've experienced so far - and perhaps for the men who are running after Christ alongside them.

- It's for those who long to use their lives to make a meaningful difference in this world.
- It's for those sitting on the pews of our churches today with untapped potential to be Kingdom players.
- And it's for those you invite to join you on your small batch adventure.

THE NUTS AND BOLTS

Small Batch Discipleship serves as both a journey and a guidebook for you to walk out biblical principles and enjoy authentic Christian community with other believers. You can expect to:

- Learn how to study your Bible on your own.
- Enjoy an intimate relationship with God in prayer.
- Share the love of Jesus Christ with those around you.
- Lead a small group community with vision and compassion.

This book is a tool to be applied within the context of real relationships. It contains all the core lessons I use with my own "small batch" discipleship groups and everything you need to know to start making disciples of Jesus who will be fully equipped to go out and do likewise.

YOUR EXPERIENCE

In order to receive the best experience from this book, I recommend the following:

1. Invite at least one other person to join you in reading this book.
2. Read each chapter on your own, and jot down any questions, ideas, or personal revelations that come to you in the margin or a journal.
3. Complete each suggested activity before continuing in your reading.
4. Look up key biblical references yourself in order to discover firsthand what God is revealing to you.
5. Gather together weekly with your partner or small group. Begin each time in prayer, and use the discussion questions at the end of each chapter to guide your conversation.
6. Remain open to opportunities for personal and spiritual growth by obeying the truths God reveals to you.

Over time, you may grow more confident teaching these core concepts yourself and prefer to use the book more like a lesson plan. That's perfectly fine! Feel free to mix in your own favorite resources and any new ideas along the way to make the experience all your own. If you catch yourself already flipping ahead through the book in search of a chart or outline of sorts, be sure to download a copy of the corresponding *Small Batch Discipleship Leader's Guide*. The guide contains a simple and customizable 6- to 12-month plan you can use to map out your next discipleship experience. Additionally, you will find pro tips for small group facilitation, helpful forms and worksheets to share with your disciples, chapter-specific bonus activities, bible memory verses, and even a coloring sheet!

YOUR INVITATION

Then the LORD replied: "Write down the revelation and make it plain on tablets, so that a herald may run with it."

Hab. 2:2 New International Version

Consider this book your official invitation to experience life with greater purpose. If you're a follower of Jesus, discipleship is what you're meant to practice forever, with whoever God places around you, wherever you go. With this book and your Bible in hand, you can begin, right now, to embrace a discipleship lifestyle you can run with for the rest of your life. Seek out a mentor or invite a friend, launch your first *Small Batch Discipleship* journey together with me, and then as Jesus says in Luke 10:37 (NIV), "go and do likewise."

introduction

Great things are done by a series of small things brought together.[1]

Vincent Van Gogh

Everything is "small batch" these days. Small batch coffee, spirits, spices, and sweets promise a taste of something beyond the ordinary. We are all drawn to this idea of something uniquely special, handcrafted, of a limited quantity, and worth experiencing. I realize this idea of small batch goodness stretches far beyond the culinary world. Small batch principles also apply to God's design for your own personal life:

- You, too, are perfectly one-of-a-kind.
- Your life story is without equal.
- A unique group of people encircle your life.
- God has handcrafted you with a special purpose in mind.
- Your time is of a limited quantity.

And, if you are a Christian, following Jesus in a Great Commission lifestyle of small batch discipleship is worth experiencing and giving the rest of your years to, whether one or ninety-one remain.

You, friend, are meant to lead others to Jesus and help them mature in their faith, all while you continue to grow in your own. More than likely, no one has shown you exactly how to do this or personally discipled you in a way that might equip you to repeat the process. Small Batch Discipleship is designed to help fill in those gaps. Ideally, the ideas presented in this book allow small batch relationships of faith to multiply, perhaps exponentially. How does this happen? Starting small, pairs of individuals or handfuls of folks gather together around sofas, coffee shops, and churches to grow closer to Jesus and one another. While the ingredients appear simple, the impact is profound. With practice and lifelong guidance from God's Word, and fellow sojourners a few steps ahead in their faith journey, we can enjoy forever the calling of God on our lives to make disciples of Jesus Christ, our impact reaching the ends of the earth until the very end of time. Let's explore together the possibility there might be more depth and complexity of flavor to this Christian experience than you've tasted so far.

COFFEE SHOP OPPORTUNITIES

> *Taste and see that the LORD is good; blessed is the one who takes refuge in him.*

> Ps. 34:8 NIV

If, like me, you are a coffee lover, you probably admire the beauty of an artisanally crafted cup of joe. Notice how a skilled barista has a true talent for creating beauty in the simple things of coffee beans, water, and milk. With plenty of practice, and guidance from master craftsmen who have gone before, they can put a signature touch on a cappuccino or latte that makes you feel as if you've been given a romantic gift. Not only do you enjoy the flavor of the coffee inside the cup, but your heart leaps a little when you observe how the shades of brown and white in the frothy cream on top become something more.

I wonder, though, how often most of us pause in our busyness and lift our eyes above the mug and rising steam to consider the person who handed us that cup. Have you ever stopped to consider the barista who handcrafted that beautiful brew, or perhaps your favorite cup of tea? What is his or her story? What has life felt like for him or her, and what happened along their life's path to shape them into the person they are today? What about other people you know and meet:

- the server at your favorite restaurant or your neighbor down the street;
- the teacher in your child's kindergarten classroom or that girl who sits next to you in homeroom;
- the person sitting next to you on the plane, or the coworker you pass near the copier each day?

God is writing each of their stories right now, too, and He has an incredible plot twist planned. That's where you come in.

Unless a Christ-follower like you or me is open to having a conversation and maybe even a relationship with them, that person may never come to personally know the One who loves them most and best. And unless we, the Church, embrace this lifestyle of Great Commission connectedness Jesus commanded and modeled, we will miss out on so much of the incredible purpose and impact God has planned for our lives. So many of us feel like there must be more to the Christian life. Truthfully, there is!

ESSENTIAL INGREDIENTS

When whipping up a small batch of handcrafted disciples, the process naturally turns out slightly different every time.

That's the beauty of how God uses your uniqueness and the Holy Spirit's intervention to do His special work in and through you. This is the art of discipleship. Meanwhile, be faithful to invest into those individuals God brings your way everything He entrusted to you along your own faith journey. Take care that every small batch experience you lead includes three essential ingredients: global impact, a strategy of multiplication, and a repeatable, systematic curriculum.

1. Global Impact

Acts 1:8 clearly states that your impact on this world for Christ is intended to reach every corner of the world, from your neighborhood to the nations. It includes reaching places outside your comfort zone and building relationships with people who are very different from you. Are you building disciples who have the entire world on their heart? (See Acts 1:8, Rom. 10:14-15, Isa. 49:6.)

2. Strategy

What was Jesus' strategy to reach the world? In studying the life of Christ, it's easy to notice He spent the majority of His time in ministry with His twelve disciples. The work of reproducing His life and earthly ministry into theirs is the "finished work" Jesus refers to in John 17:4, spoken two chapters before He took on the cross! Obviously, our redemption through His crucifixion is what Jesus references later when He said, "It is finished," in John 19:30. However, without reproducing His life into these few individuals, Jesus' redemptive work on the cross would've barely been known, and it certainly wouldn't have reached you and I today. His strategy to save the world was and is through making disciples, and our strategy to reach it has to be the very same. (See Matt. 28:18-20, John 17:4.)

One plus one makes two. Two-by-two, we become four. Four-by-four, eight, and multiplication quickly becomes the one and only way to reasonably reach the entire world for Christ. You've been chosen to multiply the life of Christ into small batch groups of individuals who will one day become ready, able, and willing to reproduce the same into others. (See 2 Tim. 2:2.)

3. Systematic Curriculum

If the process is to be duplicated, you have to give them something repeatable and applicable to any and every person God brings them to disciple. Disciple-making involves the transfer of two things from the discipler to the disciple: truth and life. (See 1 Thess. 2:8.) Truth involves a complete presentation of the foundations of the Christian faith, including the entirety of scripture and the centrality of the gospel of Jesus Christ. And life means everything beyond this, including opening the front door of your life and inviting them to come inside.

Ensure your disciples have a clear plan for what to teach and how to do it, and get them off to a great start by making certain the recipes you pass along will actually work. Rest assured everything in this book has been tried and tested over decades and across diverse cultural contexts, life stages and circumstances. With this book and your Bible, you have everything you need to begin making fellow disciples of Jesus right now, one small batch at a time.

Christianity without discipleship is always Christianity without Christ.[2]

Dietrich Bonhoeffer

This journey is more a marathon than a sprint, unfolding one small step at a time. I like to envision the discipleship process taking place in three phases:

- Exploring discipleship;
- Building the foundations of the Christian faith into practice;
- Equipping each disciple to be a Christian leader - ready to make a similar investment into someone else's life.

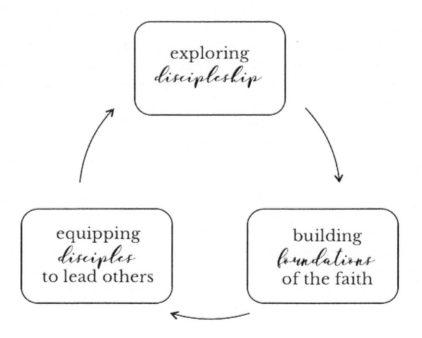

Over time, other important life lessons will naturally arise as you embrace the twists and turns of life together, such as honoring God with your habits, hobbies, body, and relation-ships. What's more, if you have the privilege of traveling abroad with your disciples, on a mission trip for example, then opportunities for real-time learning might also spring up during that experience. International travel with a small group allows growth in humility, flexibility, teamwork, appreciating your place within the context of the global Church, and developing a personal ministry network within different cultural contexts. Though not always logistically possible, this could clearly be a major lever for personal growth in Christlikeness. Meanwhile, it is always true that your best growth and learning as a disciple of Jesus comes as you are used by God to make disciples of your own. I think Jesus knew you and I would be most likely to walk out our faith in a manner worthy of the gospel (Col. 1:10, Phil. 1:27) through being held accountable to lead others. He wants us to lean in and look to *Him* to do in our disciples' lives what only *He* can do, to show up and amaze us all. This is why He calls *us* to make disciples.

KEY CONCEPTS

- A "small batch" is something unique, one-of-a-kind, handcrafted, of a limited quantity, and worth experiencing.
- You are unique. God has handcrafted you. Your time is of a limited quantity. Following Jesus in a Great Commission lifestyle of small batch discipleship is worth it.
- God's plans for you are good.
- He has called you to small batch discipleship.

my story

IN THE BEGINNING

Like any good story, I should probably start somewhere near the beginning of mine. You must know right out of the gate, I'm the least likely candidate to write this book. This book is about how amazing God is, *not* how amazing I am. I have no doubt this will be wildly clear, but let me go on record as saying, every bit of this book is about God. With that said, and with a steamy coffeehouse craft in hand, allow me to tell you my story.

I have been teaching and training leaders for more than twenty years professionally, everywhere from on ropes courses and in college classrooms to hospitals, board rooms, conferences, and even church retreats. I continue to learn more about great leadership every day, and I try to walk out the things I teach others. The truth is, though, I am a cracked pot. What I have to offer you, through *Small Batch Discipleship*, is solely the Living Water that leaks out of me and my story, and the stories of other cracked pots I've met along the way.

As a young person, neither coffee nor church were exactly my flavor, although I love both now. We didn't attend church regularly growing up, except on holidays or occasionally with other family members. Even so, I admit I found myself thinking about God often and journaling my prayers to Him throughout my adolescent years. School seemed to be my wheelhouse, and my passion in the classroom led me toward a lifetime love of learning. Once I reached university-level studies, my original pre-med coursework in biochemistry and genetics evolved, probably to my parents' chagrin, into something more closely aligned with event management and ecotourism. I moseyed off campus whenever class wasn't in session to facilitate the Alpine Tower high ropes course and lead community groups through leadership and diversity education. Honestly, that's where my heart took root, and the foundation for my career path was established.

FROM OUTWARD BOUND TO OTHERS-ORIENTED

Having finished my undergrad coursework with an extra semester to spare, I packed my bags and hopped on a plane to Central and South America to put a bow on the whole thing. My parents bravely allowed me to participate in an adventure recreation and cultural immersion program through Outward Bound. As a result, with ten other college kids and a local guide, I traipsed through jungles and climbed mountains. Our team trekked from ocean to ocean across Costa Rica, stopping along the way to stay in a Hare Krishna village, a Christian village, and another village that we were told had never hosted outsiders. Each morning, we hoisted our heavy packs up once again onto our backs, and our guide pointed out over the horizon and said, "Do you see that mountain top waaaay over there? That's where we'll stop for lunch." So, for weeks, we hiked as far as we could see, rappelled, scuba dived, and braved river rapids.

Our continued adventures took us to the waters of Panama, the breathtaking ruins of Machu Picchu, and an island homestay along Lake Titicaca in Bolivia, to name just a few. At one point, after first acclimating to the rising altitude in the nearby city of La Paz, we donned ice axes and climbing gear and made a midnight ascent of Mount Huayna Potosi to nearly twenty thousand feet. Three breaths for each step near the top, that night challenged every fiber of my being. Each of these adventures provided more than new dots on my travel map; together they truly served as a pivot point for my salvation and God's shaping of my future. The enormity of these experiences was not lost on me, but God met me in the tiniest of moments, of which two stand out.

A BIBLE IN THE JUNGLE

It took us two weeks on foot to reach a riverside village home in rural Costa Rica. The terrain was thick with shrubbery and greens, and the house, crafted simply of wooden planks nestled around large boulders on the ground. A river bubbled and sparkled along the length of the home. The scene was spectacular. This family, like the others we stayed with, survived largely off the fruit of their own land. They planted beans and yuca and tended to chickens and pigs. During one particularly memorable moment of our stay, our tree-hugging team of American suburbanites observed the slaughter of a pig during dinner preparations. Truth be told, it was one of the most horrible sights and sounds I had ever seen, and it led to hours of emotionally charged conversation. Considering we had such a hard time with the pig situation, we questioned our ability going forward to eat meat and not remember the death required to suit our appetites. Sensing our struggle, the host family gathered our small batch circle together and provided counsel. They brought out a Bible and explained that, according to scripture, God had given mankind authority over the land and animals for care-taking and for food. Regardless of the decisions each of us made for our future diets, I was dumbfounded at the bigger picture I saw in their explanation. First of all, how did they even have a Bible in this remote place? It took us weeks to reach their village. Yet, somehow their lives had clearly been organized around their faith.

As a matter of fact, theirs was the same theology I'd seen depicted in the museums and cathedrals of Europe a couple years prior, even further away. I had always been curious about world religions, but frankly I saw Christianity as a Western religion passed down from parents to their unquestioning children. A type of belief system where you were asked to blindly accept your faith without the freedom to ask difficult questions didn't settle well with my prove-it-to-me academic self. However, this experience was different. Our host family answered a difficult life question with biblical truth, steadfast peace, and conviction. I was stirred and unsettled, to say the least. What other questions might the Bible answer? And how is it this same Bible has endured time, culture, and geography the way it has?

I carried these burning questions with me as we journeyed on, and I'm sure my teammates were wrestling inside just like me. It wasn't long before we circled up once again for another deep conversation. Apparently it was time for each of us to decide where our beliefs really rested. I remember the group talking more about faith and then each person in the group answering, "What about you, do you believe in the God of the Bible?" They went one-by-one around the circle, and I was shocked as each member of my team said "yes." One yes came from a girl sent by her parents on the trip to help her kick a drug addiction. Another affirmative came from a guy who had been sleeping with another member of our team. Again, every person on our team said yes. Hypocrites! As deserving as I was to have the tables turned back on me, judgment was heavy in my heart. Sure enough, I was the last one to be asked this question. "What about you, Tracy? Do you believe in the God of the Bible?" I then spoke the words which will forever ring in my ears. "If that's what you believe, then *no*." No. No. No! It echoed in my ears. There it was, my lowest moment in life. I confessed my hatred for God aloud. I seethed with judgment, which created a hollow feeling within me. I believed in something, some kind of greater God power, but I just couldn't accept all of this. Even worse, I felt as though I declared myself an enemy of God. Looking back, it was this very moment when my rescue truly began.

God recklessly chased after me from this ugly moment on. Me. Chief of all God-haters and most prideful of sinners; the God of the Bible wanted *me*. Pastor and theologian, Tim Keller says, "The gospel is this: We are more sinful and flawed in ourselves than we ever dared to believe, yet at the very same time we are more loved and accepted in Jesus Christ than we ever dared hope."[2] More on my wrestling with God shortly. For now, I continued the journey as the captain of my own ship and with a sick, unsettled feeling in the pit of my stomach.

It was only in prior weeks my self-image had been called into question by my fellow adventurers, beyond even the call-out on my religious beliefs. As we hiked those many rainforest miles during the first part of our journey, my team brought to my attention I'd been self-centered out there. Let's be clear, the struggle was real in carrying a heavy load up steep mountain paths, bushwhacking through thick jungle foliage, and enduring long stretches of thigh-deep mud that sucked your waders off with each step. I had showered with take-your-breath-away mountain snowmelt ice water, eaten powdered milk cereal for breakfast for days, and had even gone 36 hours without food on a mini-survival solo expedition. Yet, while I fought my way through my own personal challenges, others on my team were facing struggles too, some much greater than mine. It never occurred to me I had the strength to lighten *their* loads. I pushed myself to accomplish the physical tasks before me, but nothing more. And they called me out on this. All my life, I thought I lived up so well to my maiden initials, T.L.C. (tender loving care), but sadly I realized others didn't see those same qualities shining through in my behavior. For someone who had always felt most loved through words of affirmation, that reality check stung deeply.

I rallied. Somehow I was able to swallow this trailside blow to my pride and take the next steps forward. I focused all my energy on lifting my eyes to the needs of those around me and tried to offer more of myself to serve them. I encouraged my friends when they were down and lightened their loads when they couldn't carry them anymore. I determined to slow down and accept a later stance in the group in order to help a team-mate not give up at the back of the line. I stood firm in the whitewater rapids to help others across. I learned to soften my attitude, have more fun, and be less self-important. In the stony ruins of Machu Picchu, my team presented me with a jade frog, a symbol of metamorphosis. This signified my personal growth from someone at the center of her own world into someone with selfless concern for others. I had always thought love was my greatest gift to the world, but it turned out I hadn't yet learned what it felt like to give real love away.

Love sacrifices. Love endures. Love gives. I still have that frog, and it represents an important life moment to me. I now know sometimes we have to redefine ourselves in life and become the kind of person we'd most like to be.

NORTH MEETS SOUTH

I arrived back home in Missouri, the winds blew West, and a new chapter began for me in Colorado. As I unpacked the few things that fit in the back of my old SUV and moved into my new apartment in Granby, Colorado, I wondered what the next several months would be like as I worked at a ski resort and lived with all the other seasonal employees. As it turns out, one very special liftie would soon bring a Southern splash and the gift of truth to the pages of my life story. Meanwhile, a Precious Moments® children's Bible somehow found its way into my things. I unpacked it and put it next to my bed on a small plastic crate bookshelf. While in Colorado, I found myself flipping through the pages of that children's Bible over and over in the quiet of my room, searching for answers to questions I'd never given myself permission to ask before. I'm still not really sure how that Bible got there.

I wrestled with God during those times, and I even found myself secretly visiting a nearby Christian church on the weekends. Winter came, snow set in, and my new friendship with this Southern boy, Jon, became something more. We were night-and-day different. He was a Southern Baptist kid raised in the church and was brought up searching for bullets on the old Civil War battlefields not far from Memphis, Tennessee. I was a Midwestern girl, a suburban traveler with the world in my rearview mirror and a taste for adventure. He was slow and relaxed. He loved jam bands and history. I was fast-paced and restless, and I thought I knew just about everything, well, besides history. He was a skier and I, a snowboarder. Opposites attract, of course, and God began weaving our stories together in a way only He could.

Midway through the ski season, a blizzard descended on Grand Valley and we thought it a fine time for a road trip. In all actuality, we were delivering my mom to the airport in Denver after a weekend visit. As we began making our way from the city back over the hairpin turns of Berthoud Pass, a white-out snowstorm made the trip nearly impossible. Our wipers froze; the road was invisible. We inched forward at a snail's pace for several hours, but the snow wasn't the only thing that made our journey so memorable. As we hopped back in the car that night at the airport, something compelled me to ask Jon all of the spiritual questions I'd been wrestling with. One-by-one, I hammered him with a litany of my toughest questions. One-by-one, he responded with the truths of scripture. Every question had a biblical answer, and I knew deep inside me everything he said was true. Somehow this made me really agitated inside, almost angry. Meanwhile, Jon knew his life hadn't been lining up with his faith, and the Holy Spirit brought intense conviction to him when he shared the truth he knew so well with me. For the next hour or two, neither of us could say a word. God dealt with us both in the quiet of those moments and used the other person to draw each of us closer to Him, something He continues to do today. Another layer of my rescue unfolded in that car.

The ski season eventually drew to a close when the snow finally stopped falling. Without summertime jobs, Jon and I both moved back to our hometowns. I frequently tuned the radio dial to listen in on a Memphis pastor, Dr. Adrian Rogers. As a matter of fact, I was so drawn to his messages I ended up driving down on the weekends to hear him preach in person, and of course to see Jon. It wasn't long before God won my heart. One Sunday in particular, a message I heard Dr. Rogers preach at church resonated somehow in the deepest parts of me. I felt so compelled to know the Jesus I'd once spoken out against, I could hardly sit still. I found someone at church willing to pray with me afterwards. I closed my eyes with my hands in theirs, and I asked God to forgive me and call me His own. I'm sure the words weren't pretty, and they didn't have to be, but I immediately began following Jesus.

I needed more of Jesus so I moved where God was growing me, and Memphis became my new home. Gratefully, I married that mountain man of mine not long afterward, and we set up shop right there in M-town. Blues, soul food, and Grizzlies grit-and-grind flavored the city. The scene of the church felt like it was catching fire, and God was breathing new life into all the young believers around us. God fanned a gospel flame in our hearts as a newly married couple, surrounding us with a community of friends who encouraged us and called us toward authenticity and boldness as believers. We studied God's Word and prayed together. We pursued racial reconciliation and cared for those in prison and on the streets. Ever since, the seeds of the gospel have been growing in our lives through a lifestyle of discipleship, which we'll continue to define in the chapters to come, and it remains an adventure like no other.

God has never stopped amazing Jon and I since those first snowflakes fell. Life would be so different without the many precious relationships He's added to our lives through our faith family so far - friends who have shared everything with us, from their deepest sufferings, celebrations, and discernments to our own. And looking back, it was God's hand that guided us toward those gifts, orchestrated our circumstances, and placed us right where our greatest blessings would be found.

That's my story. It's a big story, I know. In many ways, it's often felt like the things dreams are made of. But God's biggest impressions upon my heart have often been in the smallest experiences, those circles, conversations, and relationships which stuck with me. And whether your life story has been chock-full of grand adventures, or a simple string of quiet moments, I invite you to explore with me the call of Jesus. I'm guessing there might be more to this idea of discipleship than you've seen yet. I'd also guess the life God has for you just over the horizon is somehow more profound and impactful than any dream you've dreamed so far. The biggest chapters of your story will likely begin in your very own small batches.

*Now to him who is able to do immeasurably more than all we
ask or imagine, according to his power that is at work within
us, to him be glory in the church and in Christ Jesus
throughout all generations, for ever and ever! Amen.*

Eph. 3:20-21

DISCUSSION QUESTIONS

1. What are you most hoping to get out of this
   discipleship journey?
2. Discuss the concept of the small batch. What
   resonates most with you about the idea that your
   discipleship journey together will be: uniquely
   special, handcrafted, of a limited quantity, and
   worth experiencing.
3. What are some of the key milestones of your life's
   journey so far?
4. Have you ever wrestled with God or said "no" to
   God? Describe that experience.
5. Do you most often put yourself or others first?
   Share an example of a time when you've done
   both.
6. How have God's plans for your life surprised you
   or been different than your plans for yourself?

part
one

Exploring Discipleship

chapter one

Defining
discipleship

*Use me, God. Show me how to take who I am, who I want to be, and
what I can do, and use it for a purpose greater than myself.*[1]

Martin Luther King, Jr.

Amanda worked as an administrative assistant in a small
family-owned business. She struggled to find joy in life and still
hurt from a lifetime of painful experiences and relational
wreckage. While driving one day, she spotted another car
sporting a bumper sticker that advertised a local Christian
radio station, Joy FM. A single-word advertisement reflected
on the sticker, "Joy," packed a powerful punch. She thought to
herself, *Joy? I'd like to get some of that.* Seed planted.

She listened to the radio station and found encouragement
in the songs and stories shared. An on-air personality on Joy
FM had experienced a health battle with her husband. She

told listeners how she and her husband shared a meaningful spiritual conversation with the care providers at the hospital just before he passed away, and she invited listeners to watch for the people God put along their paths. Later that day, when Amanda got off work, she went to a nearby pub for happy hour with a coworker. They talked about life's hardships and frustrations, as the man at the next table listened in. When Amanda rose to leave, the neighborly eavesdropper stopped her. He asked Amanda if she'd ever considered attending church and recommended one he was familiar with. Amanda told him she'd actually been meaning to go to church for a while. Seed watered.

OUR LIVES INTERSECT

The next Sunday, she visited the church the man recommended, which happened to also be my church. Going to church was an unfamiliar experience for Amanda, but she noted the people she met were friendly, and the pastor's message seemed to speak especially to her. She also noticed a slide on the screen up front with information about an upcoming women's Bible study. Amanda thought, *I guess that's what I do next, attend Bible study*. With one foot in front of the other, she took another step.

Amanda and I met at the Bible study, where she was placed into my small group. I led an icebreaker at the start of the session. The icebreaker consisted of women tossing around a ball and sharing either (1) a description of their existing walk with Jesus or (2) if they were new to this "whole Jesus thing." Amanda chose the latter. With each passing week, Amanda discovered how studying the Bible often felt like drinking water through a fire hose. Even so, she continued to attend, observed others in the study, and listened for God's still small voice to speak to her.

At this point, God had her full attention, and she

wondered what she would do when the Bible study wrapped up. I felt compelled to invite her over to our home. A new group of women were starting the discipleship journey with me the next week, and I asked Amanda if she'd like to join us. She did. What unfolded in front of my eyes over the following months was one of the most encouraging things I've ever witnessed.

Within the small batch, Amanda discovered how God's promises applied to her own life. Without fail, she asked thought-provoking questions at every gathering. She even shared stories of her own personal childhood hurts and of friends who were struggling with very dark and heavy things. Ultimately, Amanda accepted Jesus as her Savior, believed in the gospel with her whole heart, and carried her faith boldly back into conversations with coworkers, friends, family, and everyone she met along her way. She was unashamed of the gospel, for to her it became the power of God for the salvation of everybody (Rom. 1:16). Like all of us, Amanda knew plenty of people in desperate need of Him.

Toward the end of our structured time of meeting together that year, Amanda's heart was burdened for children in foster care after temporarily taking in the child of a friend who had fallen on hard times. With a resolute spirit, she stepped forward in immediate obedience to the Lord by taking a class to become a certified foster parent. She saved up, bought a house so she'd have enough space for others, and welcomed two precious little boys into her home and heart as her first foster care placement. Today, they are on track to become adopted, forever members of Amanda's family.

I stand amazed! Amanda's story brings my heart over-whelming inspiration and conviction. Her life is pure evidence of God's transforming work and overflowing grace in this world. Her focus on the Lord is real, raw, and genuine. Her prompt obedience and boldness of faith are inspiring. This friend of mine makes me believe in my God more fully and also makes me want to take a leap of obedience as I follow God toward whatever marvelous works He has ahead for me.

THE BIGGER PICTURE

What's the bigger picture and purpose Jesus had in mind when He wrote each of our life stories? I think all of us at some point ask questions like, "Why am I here?" and, "Why is this happening to me?" You may be asking, for that matter, why should I consider taking on a discipleship lifestyle when I already have more than enough on my plate to keep me running ragged into infinity? Furthermore, why now?

We hear the word "discipleship" used in so many ways in our churches today, and I'm afraid most of us are more than a little fuzzy on its actual meaning. Does discipleship mean attending church on Sundays and perhaps even dropping some money into the offering plate or basket as it passes by? Does it mean being present in our church bubbles every Sunday morning to hear sermons and Wednesday nights for additional studies? Perhaps discipleship is about showing up throughout the week for church-based sports, musical activities, and meals? Or maybe it means going to Bible studies and community groups and serving in the church nursery? Delivering casseroles to church members with new babies? Making coffee or directing traffic? No, I suggest it means something more. Something else.

Let me be clear, those aren't bad things. As a matter of fact, I think our experience within the local church setting is vitally important as members of the Body of Christ, and helping to create a sacred space for others to encounter God is nothing shy of a mighty work. Meanwhile, I dare to suggest that discipleship for a Christian is, in fact, simpler. Discipleship means literally *being* a personal disciple, or a student and follower, of Jesus. Discipleship is all about living our lives *like*

Jesus and *with* Jesus. This requires taking a long, hard look at what Jesus actually said and did with His life.

Jesus came to earth, after all, to seek and save the lost (Luke 19:10). He brought the truth about God's plan of salvation for all people, the good news we call the gospel. He showed us the heart and face of God, and He called those of us who follow Him to use our lives for a very special and specific purpose: to make fellow disciples out of those who need Him, from our nearest neighbors to people in every nation. As followers of Jesus Christ, we are all called to obey the command of the Great Commission, to take up a discipleship lifestyle within our own unique context. During His final moments of life on earth, following His resurrection and just before His heavenly ascension, Jesus purposely selected His final words to humanity. Christ left no doubt of the divine importance of these final utterances. Let's look a little closer at a modern day example of *just* that.

I love the movie, *The Proposal*.[2] It's a romantic-comedy, and I could watch it again and again. In the movie, a female executive book publisher has a male assistant. Their relationship is tumultuous, to say the least. But as with any good chick flick, romance and humor bloom in the end. They venture together to the guy's hometown in Alaska to visit his family, and they eventually get married to secure her American citizenship. Conflict between the assistant and his dad threatens to sever the family bonds, so his grandmother stages her own heart attack to pull them back together. As a helicopter comes to carry grandma into town for treatment, the male protagonist and his dad stand over their beloved matriarch, hanging on her every last word. What words of wisdom will be so important that she uses her very last breaths to speak? The grandmother imparts wisdom about the importance of family. The men take her words to heart, they come back together, and she immediately arises and returns to her normal self. Fake emergency averted. Every time I watch this movie, as funny as it is, I'm reminded of the potential far-reaching impact of our words to others. They can breathe life and harmony into the world, and they can cause division and pain. Moreover, I'm reminded that someone's parting words at the moment of death will likely stick with their family members forever. They can either bless or haunt the lives of those they leave behind, and they might even affect how their loved ones live the rest of their own lives after they are gone.

> *Then Jesus came to them and said, "All authority in heaven and on earth has been given to me. Therefore go and make disciples of all nations, baptizing them in the name of the Father and of the Son and of the Holy Spirit, and teaching them to obey everything I have commanded you. And surely I am with you always, to the very end of the age."*
>
> Matt. 28:18-20

These were the parting words of Jesus! These are the words He used His last breaths to express to us, our marching orders, and it's what we know today as the Great Commission. We'll dig into these words more shortly, but for now may the final words of Jesus stick with us forever as God's family members. May they bless us and cause us to steer our lives accordingly until He comes again. May we keep on following Christ by exponentially making His disciples. And may He gain all the glory.

I realize how your mind naturally starts to spin when you read or hear something like this, so let's solidify our definition of discipleship. What are the specifics of how this all plays out in our lives today? Stick with me and pray continually that God will illuminate His Word and His intentions for you as we go.

DEFINING DISCIPLESHIP

A. W. Tozer once said, "Only a disciple can make a disciple." So then, what *makes* a person a disciple? Furthermore,
what does *making* a disciple actually involve? Simply put, the
Merriam-Webster Dictionary defines a disciple as a student,
follower, adherent, apprentice or protégé. As a *student* and
follower, you can't double major in following Jesus and chasing
after selfish ambitions. Therefore, being a true disciple of Jesus
Christ means learning from Him, believing in Him with your
whole heart and life, and following in the teacher's footsteps. A
disciple is also an *adherent*, attached like adhesive tape to the
Teacher, sticking with Jesus and covered with the residue of
His grace. An *apprentice* selects a vocation, studies and learns
from their mentor, and then assumes the master's work. So
too, a disciple spends time with Jesus, studies and mirrors His
example, and forsakes every other kind of lifestyle for His.

I once saw a long-tailed manakin, a fairly common bird
species in Costa Rica with black, blue, and red feathers that
puts on a stunning show of apprenticeship. For seven to ten
years, a young male apprentice will partner with an older,
alpha male bird to learn an intricate and graceful mating
dance, which the two will one day perform together to attract
a mate for the master. They practice for years, one ballet-like
movement on top of the next, until finally the day comes
when they're ready to dance before the female. The mentor's
chance to successfully breed fully depends upon the presence
and contributions of the protégé. If they work together, if
their relationship and skills are harmonious, multiplication will
result. And one day, when the mentor is gone, his wingman
will be ready to do likewise.

Fortunately, we don't have to wait a decade to assume our
Master's work. But the similarities are overwhelming between
this wonder of nature and the dance of discipleship. Rather
than competing, we too are called to pair up to multiply the
life of Christ in this world. As disciples of Jesus, you and I pair

up with one another, practice together the skills required to live out our Christian faith, and perform them among a watching world. If our relationships with God and with one another are harmonic, Kingdom growth will result!

A TWO-WAY STREET

I've always loved running the rural roads near our home - hilly, winding roads that bicyclists also adore. One sunny afternoon, I went for a long jog. I made it three quarters of the way along my route when I hit a wall. The spring was gone from my step, and I thought very seriously about calling it a day. About that time, a team of road bikers headed toward me on the other side of the street. They shouted, "Way to go, runner! You're doing great!" It was just what I needed to finish strong. I mustered up enough energy to return the favor, "Good ride, y'all!" After all, they had just crested a major hill climb and still had smiles all over their faces. It was lucky for me that my route was along a two-way street. Without the enthusiastic encouragement from those others-oriented passersby, my push to the finish line might have ended quite differently that day.

Discipleship is also a two-way street. As a disciple, you cultivate a friendship with God by spending time with Him, just as you do with your other friends. You hang out together by soaking up His Word and relishing conversation with Him through prayer. Your faith is made stronger through the encouraging presence of other believers, just like my band of bikers. Because you're wild about this Friend of yours, the words you speak are often about Him, which means the love of God reaches people around you who need it. As you grow spiritually, Jesus pours His life into you until you are so full it splashes over onto those around you. In that overflow, through a Great Commission lifestyle of handcrafted, small batch disciple-making relationships, you build up other disciples of Jesus while you yourself continue growing.

Honestly, this is where things get interesting with discipleship. When you are accountable to spiritually leading another person, you're more likely to legitimately do those life practices you know you ought to be doing. For example, you teach them to be students of the Bible, and so you remember to study yours. You encourage them to take everything to the Lord in prayer, which reminds you He's there to talk with you, too. You open yourself up to them, and they return the investment tenfold by sharing with you their own wisdom, experiences, and perspective. Certainly, the blessings flow both ways. You better believe Jesus knew from the very beginning how invaluable this cooperative journey would be for our own growth.

On the grounds the Great Commission was originally spoken and recorded in Greek, the popular language of Jesus' day, it's worth our time to examine the actual words Jesus chose when He gave us this important charge and what He really meant as He uttered such impactful words. Rudyard Kipling, an English writer, author of *The Jungle Book*, said, "I keep six honest serving-men (They taught me all I knew); Their names are What and Why and When and How and Where and Who."′ Let's put on our literary hats and apply Kipling's timeless questions to thoroughly grasp the implications of Christ's call on our lives.

THE WHO

Let's start with the "who." *Who* did Jesus command in the Great Commission? The verses that follow here are addressed to "ye" in the King James translation of the Bible, the plural word meaning you all. I'd say, "you guys" if I were speaking to my midwestern friends and a nice warm "y'all," or even "all

y'all," to my tribe in the steamy South. Jesus spoke here to all
His committed followers, and this includes you and me today.

You may have heard it asked before (an awful saying for
any horse-loving girl like me): What's the fastest way to kill a
horse? The answer: have two people assigned to feed it. I can
attest to this with regard to assigning kids to feed fish. If each
of my children thinks the other is going to feed our fish,
inevitably they either get overfed or left eating bubbles. In
essence, if we each think the other person is responsible for
something, neither of us is likely to be reliable to do it. By the
same standard, who is responsible for fulfilling the Great
Commission? All of us! However, if we think in those terms,
we are no different than the figurative people assigned to feed
the horse. Rather, I need to recognize it as *my* responsibility in
the same way *you* own the commission for yourself. If asked,
each of us can boldly say the Great Commission was given to
me! Who is going to carry out the Great Commission? *I am!*

Perhaps, like many others, you assume this is the responsibility of pastors and other church staff. After all, they are the
'professionals'. On the contrary, our pastors exist to build up
the saints (you and me) for the work of the ministry (Eph.
4:11-13). While, again, I think it's crucial for Christ-followers
to be part of a local church family, let's remember the early
Christian church wasn't even created until *after* Jesus' ascension, when He spoke those parting words, and first denoted
biblically in Acts chapter two. No, the Great Commission was
not intended to primarily be a responsibility of church staff or
lived out from behind the pulpit. Rather, it is for all believers.
Throughout the New Testament, we see early believers gathered into small batch communities, allowing for greater
engagement and responsibility of each Christ-professing
member. They lived out their faith and shared all about the
Lord with people they knew and met; some linked arms with
them and became a part of the family of God. The Great

Commission then, in actuality, was a charge given to run-of-the-mill people, just like you and me.

Jesus focused on a chosen few from the very beginning, His committed disciples. Pastor and best-selling Christian author, Max Lucado, expresses it well, "A man who wants to lead the orchestra must turn his back on the crowd."[5] It's an unconventional concept, yet it's exactly what we see Jesus doing during His earthly ministry. After His preaching and healing works among the people, Jesus made a habit of dismissing the masses, stealing away, and pouring deeply and intentionally into His few, knowing ultimately this was the only way to truly reach and save the rest of humanity in the end. If we peek ahead from the mountaintop to Acts 1:8 and 8:1-4, we see the good news propelled out to the people of the world by laypersons. Again, Jesus intended to reach the world through commonplace, everyday individuals like you and me. This is our calling to embrace.

> *Then Jesus came to them and said, "All authority in heaven and on earth has been given to me. Therefore go and make disciples of all nations, baptizing them in the name of the Father and of the Son and of the Holy Spirit, and teaching them to obey everything I have commanded you. And surely I am with you always, to the very end of the age".*

Matt. 28:18-20

THE WHAT

With these instructions, *what* exactly are we supposed to be doing? Let me give you a brief assignment. Read our Great Commission verses above once more. How many verbs, or action words, do you see within the passage? Did you find three or four? More? Seven is the correct answer, but of those seven there are actually only *four* main active verbs:

- Go
- Make (disciples)
- Baptize
- Teach

Of these four verbs, "make disciples" is the only true imperative (a command). If I had a room filled with people and asked them to shout out the *one* command found in the Great Commission, I can almost guarantee ninety-nine percent of people would all shout out in a rowdy, unified voice, "Go!" Smiling, yet just as emphatically, would be my response, "Guess again." More on "go" in just a moment. The one command is *matheteuo* in the original Greek (μαθητεύω), which means to be a disciple, to make disciples, to teach and instruct.[6] The original language tells us a ton about this word's meaning. It's an aorist tense, active and imperative verb, meaning the verb occurs either in the past or indefinitely, involves action, and is a requirement or command. That was a mouthful, so consider reading that last sentence again. Because you cannot command someone to do something already past, we consequently know this action exists without a time frame. Therefore, we are to make disciples always and actively. It's not an optional exercise.

As we learn to love God with all our heart, soul, mind, and strength (Mark 12:30), we are also to love our neighbors, invite others along, and pursue the Lord together. What does this practically look like?

- We meet people right where they are as our lives intersect with theirs.
- We care for the hurting and those in need by giving of ourselves: our resources, time, and attention.

- We share the good news of the gospel with them as we care for them.
- Finally, we pour ourselves out completely on their behalf and journey together in seeking to love, honor, and obey God.

...Just like Jesus did. Just like His first disciples did. And in this kind of faith-filled, relational living, He promised to be with us. *This* is discipleship. Disciples are lifelong learners and followers of Jesus. Disciples of Jesus Christ make other disci-ples of Jesus Christ.

The Christian life is the discipled life and the discipling life.[7]

Mark Dever

THE WHEN

When should we be making disciples? We learned moments ago that making disciples is something we are to do *all* the time. Let's also reflect back on the word "go" from earlier for more on this. In the Great Commission, the word "go" in the original Greek aorist, reflects a word in a passive participle tense. (Hang with me a bit longer as I break this down. I know your eyes might be glossing over.) This means "go" occurs, once again, in the past or without a time frame; *not* something to actively do, but rather more of a describing word. Unknow-ingly, many in the church cling to that word "Go" and stand ready with suitcases packed to head somewhere exotic in pursuit of the call of Christ. While we'll see that God is indeed calling us to take His good news everywhere, in reality this descriptive foreword to the command translates more like "as you are going" or even "having gone." That's surprising, right? So then, now we see Jesus' words actually translate, "As you are going (wherever you are going today), make disciples." Heading to work or school? Make disciples. Pushing a stroller to the playground where there are other moms or dads? Make disciples. Flying overseas on business, or maybe caring for others in a hospital bed? Make disciples. All the time, we are to fill our hearts to overflowing with the goodness of Jesus, to share Him with others, and to invite them along with us as we pursue Christ. Rinse and repeat.

THE WHERE

Where do we do this? Is our discipleship ministry limited to our homes, the playground, or our office place? The Great Commission verse in Matthew instructs us to make disciples of *all* nations. Acts 1:8 captures it this way, "But you will receive power when the Holy Spirit comes on you; and you will be my witnesses in Jerusalem, and in all Judea and Samaria, and to the ends of the earth." This sentence places equal and simultaneous emphasis on all of these locations: our nearest neighborhoods and towns, outside the township, across the tracks, and over the big pond. Keep in mind, Matthew 13:38 specifies "the field" where we are to fling the seeds of the gospel "is the world." Jesus indeed expects His followers to carry His movement to every nation and people group on this great planet.

In 2020, the Joshua Project identified 17,424 people groups in the world. Of those people groups, 7,410 (42.5%) were considered unreached with the gospel.[8] Hence, if someone in those lands wanted to know about Jesus Christ, there would be no Christian presence and no Bible available to help them, making outside Christian assistance necessary. Even to those unreached places, we are expected to take the message of the hope of the gospel.

This huge global application of the command of Jesus often feels (rightly) overwhelming. How on earth could one person like you or me make disciples of all nations? Before you throw in the towel, remember scripture is filled with statements about God's heart for the nations. If this is God's mission, He will accomplish it. As for each of us, Jesus invites you and me to join Him in what He is *already* doing all across the globe. Psalm 2:8 (English Standard Version) states, "Ask of me, and I will make the nations your inheritance, the ends of the earth your possession." Sometimes He even brings the nations right into your own backyard.

As a matter of fact, we once had a neighbor move in next door from China, and her family came over to the US to visit for months at a time. Our friendship was important to me, and we spent lots of time together. Our homes were wide open to one another, so much so that, unbeknownst to me, my dog regularly ran in to greet them in the mornings when I let him outside. Apparently he has a life all his own! Over time, I taught my neighbor friend how to change diapers, and she taught me how to make killer fried rice. Most importantly, we talked about God. So believer, take heart. Sometimes God will take you to the nations, and sometimes He will bring the nations to you. Consider this challenge: put your "yes" on the table, and allow God to move it across the map. Be willing to embrace being uncomfortable, and be intentional about forming relationships with people who are different than you in every way. Start small, pray big, and watch God light your heart on fire for *all* of His people, both near and far away.

THE HOW

How exactly do we make disciples? If we refer back to those four main verbs, the Great Commission of Jesus says to (#1) *make* disciples in these ways: *going* (#2), *baptizing* (#3), and *teaching* (#4). *Make* disciples as you are going along in life.

We're always going, am I right? Wherever you are going, God has placed people there. Put your spiritual antennae up. Be on the lookout for spiritually meaningful conversations and relationships wherever you are *going* as you do life. Next, make disciples by *baptizing* new believers and by helping followers of Jesus go deeper in their faith walk. Baptism represents our identification with Christ. Physical immersion in the waters of baptism helps us identify ourselves with the death, burial, and resurrection of Jesus Christ. Once we become a true believer, we also die to our old ways of life and are given a new life in Christ Jesus. As a discipler of others, you'll help them continually deepen and define their own Christian identities. Finally, make disciples by *teaching* them to read and obey the word of God. This calling, by the way, is for all of us and not just for those who feel they are "gifted" teachers.

I love to teach. As a matter of fact, it's been my primary life's work in one shape or another since I was a teenager. My first jobs were teaching gymnastics and swimming lessons. Then, as you know, I went to college and began teaching leadership workshops and climbing techniques on the ropes course, as well as leadership and diversity education to peers in the classroom. Over the years since, teaching has remained a great passion of mine. Today, I teach discipleship and Bible studies and co-lead my daughter's girl scout troop. I'm teaching my son to swim, and during the day I coach managers and executives on leadership strategy and best practices. I love to teach and encourage others. I realize, though, having partnered with all different types of people, there's a good chance this might not be your comfort zone; even so, Jesus still said for *you* to do it. What this tells me is He intends to impart His truth using *you* and your unique voice and giftings in order to bless those people He has placed in *your* sphere of influence. You, friend, are therefore to *teach* those He brings you. The amazing news is God will empower and equip you to do this if you will only seek Him.

You can give without loving, but you cannot love without giving. [9]

Dr. Adrian Rogers

When He brings them, study on your disciples' behalf by using this book and others that bless you. Pray earnestly for God to reveal Himself to them through His Word and through you in ways you couldn't do on your own. Above all, be patient. This takes time and intentionality. Discipleship is costly. You'll invest time to study, pray, prepare, and meet with your disciples when you'd otherwise be doing something else. This is a loving thing to do. It may cost you financially as you share your material resources with others in need or travel to share God's Word with people groups far away. It will cost you your pride as you open up to others about your own struggles and failures in life and invite your disciples to pray for you and encourage you in the same way you do for them. It will certainly cost you some TV time, and even time away from your family and friends. But, it will be worth it in the end.

Over a century ago, William Dallman proclaimed, "If Christ is worth anything, He is worth everything." It remains today. Your sacrificial investment into the lives of others will not come back to you empty. It's truthfully baked into the process. Your disciples will raise questions you didn't think to ask, and you'll explore truth together to find the answers. You will be held accountable to engage in the daily practices that grow your own faith as you ask your disciples to do them too. They'll share examples of what God is doing in their hearts and lives that will inspire your faith in ways you'd miss out on otherwise. And your family and friends will be blessed through your character growth and in knowing you're giving of yourself to be a blessing to others. In every way, your emotional and spiritual tank will be made full as you embrace this selfless adventure - going, baptizing, and teaching.

Making disciples of Jesus is the overflow of our delight in being disciples of Jesus. [10]

David Platt

When I began meeting with my first two disciples, one of them shared with me later that she initially came to my house with a Bible and an index card. She had planned to capture spiritual "zingers," as she called them, to inspire her later. Fast forward a year or two down the road when she began meeting with her own disciple, my phone rang and these were the words I heard on the other end of the line, "Tell me everything again, and start from the beginning." When we are accountable to teach truth to someone else, we take it more seriously. We want to get it right and to rightly understand what we are teaching. We want to experience the truth personally so we have something valuable to share with the other person. This is my favorite part of the process. When you see your disciple begin to really *get* the truths you've invested into them, and even to share them with someone else, the reward is completely life-giving.

THE WHY

Why bother doing all of this? First and foremost, we do it because Jesus said to. We do it because Jesus did it. We make disciples because it benefits us personally. We do it because it's the greatest thing we can do with our lives for the Kingdom of God.

As noted earlier, don't we already have enough on our

plates to keep us busy in life? Maybe you've heard of the "Yes, And" exercise that improv artists use to inspire their own creativity and collaboration. *Yes*, all of us seem to have more than enough on our plates to keep us busy, *and* making space in our lives to relationally and spiritually come alongside others is critically important. *Yes*, we've all got the same 525,600 minutes in any given year. No more, no less. *And*, we do *make time* for what is truly important to us. If your experience proves to be anything like mine, once you enjoy the depth and authenticity of relationships with other disciples in a small batch community of faith, nothing else will satisfy. When you are no longer meeting regularly, you'll long for more of this genuine fellowship and your own intimacy with Christ, and you'll be ready to start again with someone else at once. It's just that good.

We've gone through the who, what, when, where, how, and why of the Great Commission. You get it now. This is *way* bigger than collecting spiritual zingers. It's bigger than simply serving on Sunday. It's, in fact, the primary way Jesus plans to reach and transform the people around you with His truth and love. If you seek Him in this calling, *your* people will come. Maybe they're already right in front of you.

MEET HERB

My husband, Jon, works in healthcare. Many years ago, he worked as a nuclear medicine technologist and often provided organ scans for patients with potentially serious medical issues, in an effort to help their doctors land on a diagnosis. One Friday morning, Jon went into work with the concept of making disciples swirling around in his heart and mind. It so happened that Wednesday night he attended a men's Bible study in which the speaker explored, through scripture, the command of Jesus to His followers to make disciples. If this was true, Jon wondered, how was it possible for him to have grown up in the church and never heard this before nor seen it played out in day-to-day life? I know this is precisely what many of you might be thinking as well. He wrote to a friend, "If God is serious about this, He's going to have to show me." Show him, He did. Jon's last patient that Friday was Herb.

Like all of Jon's patients, Herb had every reason to come in that day worried and distracted by his own circumstances. By contrast, Herb walked into Jon's office and spotted the open Bible on his desk and inquired about it. Jon proceeded to talk with Herb about the Lord and, specifically, about this idea of discipleship he'd been turning around in his mind.

A two-hour procedure stretched into four. Herb listened, asked questions, and Jon rambled. Jon explained discipleship to a man who led countless disciples stretching all across the globe to follow Christ. Herb pastored for thirty-something years and left that role to focus on training others to make disciples themselves. He had written dozens of books on this topic in addition to Bible studies. Still, Herb simply listened to Jon.

Near the end of their time together, Herb mentioned Jon's stories were so captivating and asked if he would like to join him and a group of men meeting together Friday night. Jon noted his in-laws, my family, were coming into town to stay with us, so he wasn't able to attend. Not a problem, Herb added, as there was another group meeting at his house at 5:00 a.m. on Tuesday, and he wondered if Jon would like to come then. As a result, Jon's 5:00 a.m. discipleship journey began.

For the first time in our married life, he popped up hours before work or school required him to and my hubby trekked across town to sit at Herb's side to learn and grow. The group actually turned out to be a collection of pastors, with Jon the only lay-person and several decades younger than all the other men. After some time, Herb asked Jon if he'd like to start coming over an hour earlier than the rest of the group so they could have extended one-on-one time. As you might guess, their 4:00 a.m. experience meeting together flipped Jon's life upside down in all the best ways (and therefore mine as well), and it wasn't long before the two of them were taking these same truths to share with pastors and lay people all around the world.

Jon brought home everything he learned and shared it with me. He taught the very same things Herb taught him to the Sunday school class we were leading at church. While at work, Jon shared about God with his patients and coworkers whenever possible. Jon's behavior, passion for the Lord, and purpose in life were all transformed through Herb's shepherd-like love. Looking back, the trajectory of our marriage, our family, and our entire future changed that Friday afternoon. And to think, Herb might have understandably focused entirely on his own health that day. Rather, "as you are going, make disciples..."

KEY CONCEPTS

- The Great Commission: who, what, when, where, how, and why
- God's purpose for your life should be the "why" behind everything you do.
- A disciple is a lifelong learner and follower of Jesus.
- Disciples make other disciples.
- You make time for what's truly important to you.

DISCUSSION QUESTIONS

1. Do you feel like there might be more to the Christian life than what you've experienced so far?

2. Why do you think the words Jesus spoke in Matthew 28:18-20, known as the "Great Commission," were the final words Jesus chose to say to His followers?

3. Based on the definition found in this chapter, would you describe yourself as a disciple of Jesus Christ? Why or why not?

4. Review the "who, what, when, where, how, and why" of the Great Commission. In what ways does this explanation help you better understand Jesus' expectations for you as His disciple?

5. What fears or concerns do you have about teaching others, if any?

6. Do you agree you make time for the things most important to you? Explain. What is one way you can start freeing up time in your life to live out the Great Commission?

chapter two

Discipleship is
relationship

Only connect!...Live in fragments no longer. [1]

E. M. Forster

As a general rule when seeking potential disciples to partner with, look for people around you who know the least about Jesus *and* those who are the hungriest for more: more of God and more life purpose. Gathering both types of people into your inner circle might mean your small batch could include Sunday school attendees alongside others who've never set foot inside a church building, and that's okay. As a matter of fact, it's better than okay. Don't exclude anyone from your mental list of potential small batch co-adventurers.

The beauty of the small batch is how God often gathers

diverse individuals together, with each person's individuality adding a layer of depth to the community shared together. So far, it's also been true in my own experience that each participant's journey to our discipleship circles has been just as unique as the individual.

MEET LAUREN

Lauren, a hard-charging, country girl, was a junior in high school and part of the youth group of our local church in Memphis, Tennessee. At one point, Jon and I led Sunday night small groups with the high schoolers, and that's where we met. Lauren and I enjoyed a special connection, and I soon invited her into our home to help with babysitting our kids. Lauren observed our lives up close, and she took note of how we interacted with our kids. She witnessed us share the gospel with strangers and serve those in need in our community, and she heard stories about God's activity in our lives through discipleship.

Time passed, and Lauren headed off to college after graduating high school. Jon and I had our third baby, and a few months elapsed since my last group of disciples launched out to make disciples of their own. The swirl of life with two toddlers and a newborn settled down somewhat for me, and I missed the special relationship, spiritual encouragement, and accountability of having my Jesus tribe around. I woke up early one morning and cried out to the Lord during my quiet time. In prayer, I admitted to God I was feeling spiritually lonely and asked Him to bring me a new disciple to walk with. The wildest thing happened! As I wrapped up around 5:30 or 6:00 a.m., I checked my social media account and had a direct message waiting in my inbox. Lauren actually messaged me around midnight the night before, "Hey, Mrs. Tracy. This summer I will be leading a Bible study with some of the girls I have become close to throughout the semester. But it's hard to pour into the life of another when you're not being poured into yourself, so I was wondering if you would be interested in discipling me or if you even have time in your schedule to disciple me?" Oh my gosh! Was I honestly reading this correctly? Was the time stamp on that message correct? She and I hadn't talked in months, but through her request God amazingly answered my prayer *before* I even asked Him.

Our relationship grew deeper from that point on, and Lauren truly became a part of our family, much like a daughter. We spent hours and hours at the feet of Jesus together and countless late nights sitting up with Jon and her boyfriend, Spencer, on the couch chatting about marriage and dreaming about their future. We cheered Lauren along as she discipled several high school girls through Young Life. We watched as one of them moved overseas to share Christ with an Arabic nation because of the way Lauren loved to study Arabic. How inspiring! All three of our kids walked down the aisle the day she and Spencer got married: this down-to-earth farm girl who charges boldly into the most awkward conversation and her rugby-playing warrior who dedicated his life to be by her side forever. We treasured their stories about sharing Jesus with their neighbors and loving others well through their work.

Sadly, we also stood on their front porch and helped them bear the immense weight of grief just hours after they lost their infant son, Martin. Through discipleship we have been privileged to share in their heights of joy and depths of sadness. Although this pain was something none of us ever imagined all those years earlier, I know God will flood them with light and life in the coming years. We want to be on the front porch for all those moments too.

The best thing to hold onto in life is each other.[2]

Audrey Hepburn

MEET BARRETT

We moved to my hometown of St. Louis after twelve years
of calling Memphis home. Initially, we were unsure why God
called us to the city known as the "Gateway to the West"
instead of back to the Rocky Mountains *out* west. Not surprisingly, it wasn't long before God revealed His plan included us
meeting some extremely precious people on this next segment
of our life's journey. Jon met a dear new disciple, Barrett, not
long after we moved. Barrett and Jon had mutual connections
from Memphis, and they became fast friends.

Much like Lauren did earlier, Barrett became an intimate
part of our family and home. In study and prayer, he and Jon
spent considerable time at the feet of Jesus together. We
chatted into the early morning hours on the couch, and we
cheered Barrett on from the friends-and-family section of the
football field, which was where he worked his day job. He
wrestled our kids like a giant bear, helped us tuck them in, and
talked openly with them about loving the Lord. They prayed
for Barrett like a brother and remain proud to know him, to
this day. After a year or so of their one-on-one discipleship
journey, Barrett invited a few NFL teammates to join him in
his weekly time with Jon. My grocery bill doubled, but thankfully, so did the life and presence of the Holy Spirit in our
home. As Jon invested life and truth into his guys, they were,
in turn, an enormous blessing to Jon and our entire family. It
didn't take long before the married men in the group brought
their wives along to join in on the fun.

MEET KIMBERLY AND CASE

An inspiration from the first moment I met her, Kimberly captured my admiration immediately, as she exuded optimism, romance, and loyalty. Her love for the Lord, the way she adored her husband, Case, and her passion for adventure were quite evident the more I grew to know Kimberly. For several weeks, while the guys met upstairs in the "Upper Room" above our garage, Kimberly and I spent time jogging together, playing with our kids and getting them ready for bedtime, and connecting about life. I invited her to consider joining my ladies discipleship group, which met on another evening of the week. She was initially reluctant to spend an evening away from Case during the football season, when their time together was already at a premium.

One night, however, while sitting on our back porch with the melodies of crickets and pond frogs in the background, our conversation turned toward the Great Commission and discipleship. Kimberly wondered aloud how it was possible to have grown up in the church, like she did, and yet never hear about regular, everyday people making disciples in their day-to-day context like she witnessed with Jon and me. We wrestled through that question together with tears and vulnerability. That night, God ignited a new passion in Kimberly to learn as much as possible about how to replicate this for other women going forward.

We only had a few short months left together at this point, as the St. Louis Rams soon became the Los Angeles Rams and off they moved to California, but we made the most of every minute together. I loaded all the teaching, real-life stories, and insights about making disciples I could into those few months we had left, trusting God to equip her and fill in any gaps I left behind. And then, almost without warning, God launched them out to their next chapter of football life.

Given the compressed timeline, our relationship made me realize the urgency of discipleship and living on mission during every season of life. After all, aren't we all living on borrowed time? If today were your last, would you have made the very most of every conversation and every opportunity to pour into the people around you and point them to Jesus?

Over the course of the next three or four years, we watched Case and Kimberly from many miles away share Christ in the locker room, on the field, on TV, behind microphones, over radio airwaves, in their home, and even at the gym. Kimberly quickly built relationships with players' wives and with neighbors in every city God led them to, strategically and intentionally making disciples as God moved them across the map.

God can use each one of us, whatever our unique place and platform in the world. He uniquely equips and uses the administrative assistant, the executive, the professional athlete or pro spouse, stay-at-home parent, teacher, student, single person, married couple, and everyone in between. When you seek God with all your heart and commit to following His lead in a Great Commission lifestyle of making disciples of Jesus, He attracts others to Himself like a magnet through you. Pray for a disciple. Keep seeking Christ. Keep talking with others about all God is showing you in your discipleship adventures, and keep inviting others to join you. At just the right time and in just the right ways, watch the Holy Spirit move, and see God write stories all around you that you get to joyfully tell for a lifetime.

GROWING THE CONNECTION

Once you have formed an initial connection with your new small batch, take care to create a gathering space when you're together where that connection can grow. It's important everyone in your small batch feels safe to ask their toughest questions, to share where they are feeling stuck or unsure, and to be their authentic self with the group.

In her book, *The Art of Gathering³*, Priya Parker reminds us that gathering is meaning making. She encourages each of us to think carefully about the purpose every time we gather a group of individuals together. Once we know it, we need to protect that purpose by clearly articulating it to those invited and by "generously excluding" anyone not bought-in to fully participating. Priya encourages hosts of gatherings large and small to "make your purpose your bouncer;" in doing so, you're actually protecting the experience of those who really want to be there. With this in mind, feel free to invite anyone along into your discipleship adventure who shows interest or who God puts on your heart. Meanwhile, if something is getting in the way of the group dynamic or preventing inter-personal safety, you need to have a courageous conversation with the person(s), or humbly and lovingly give anyone who's not fully committed permission to leave until they're able to truly be all-in.

I've had to remind myself on multiple occasions over the years it's okay to love a lukewarm disciple and let her leave the group if that's what's best for her and your group at the time. In such a case, continue being a great friend, keep the invitation open should something change in the future, and keep at it with your small batch. Remember, even many of Jesus' own disciples turned back from following Him when they realized the cost of discipleship. But for those whom God has turned on the light switch regarding discipleship, wild horses can't keep them away.

When I think about the type of disciples we invite in and the kind we are focused on becoming, I am reminded of tacos, but not the food truck kind. In this case, T.A.C.O. represents an acronym.

- **T**eachable
- **A**vailable
- **C**ommitted
- **O**thers-oriented

Each of us, as *teachable* disciples of Jesus, need to remain humble enough to receive instruction and wisdom from others and to have someone else speak into our life. We need to stay curious and remain lifelong learners. We should make ourselves *available* to God and to other people, opening the front door of our life to them. We can't be too busy to make space for this gathering time and for new relationships. Remember, there's no "busy bee award" distributed when we arrive in Heaven. We need to *commit* to run with this new life-style Jesus calls us to for as long as He gives us life and breath. Finally, we want to be others-oriented, not dominated by solely focusing on ourselves, but rather on loving others and making a positive difference in the world around us.

Honestly, none of us is going to be all four of these things right out of the gate or on any given day without fail. I know I'm not. Even so, these are the qualities you need to nurture in one another. Doing so will reveal which of your disciples is likely to keep running with Jesus and actually repeat the investment into others when the time comes, which is where your investment will count the most. Coincidentally, if you happen to gather together with your small batch on Tuesdays, all the better! You'll have a brand new "T.A.C.O. Tuesday" tradition. If it happens to be a day other than Tuesday when you gather, well, who's to say that every day can't be the perfect one for a taco?

Priya also shares in her book how purposeful beginnings and endings to our gatherings shape personal experiences and form lasting memories. According to experts, we set the cultural norms for our group within the first five percent of our time together. Meanwhile, what participants most remember about any gathering after they leave are the final moments. So, within your small batch, you might think about starting and concluding your group with prayer, by lighting a candle, with a call-and-response statement, a creative icebreaker, playing music, or some other special tradition which feels meaningful to your group.

Finally, according to *The Art of Gathering*[4], truly transformative gatherings include some measure of risk or "heat." Considering the discipleship process should be both transformational and informational, don't avoid difficult conversations and questions that arise along the way. Remember, you aren't expected to have all the answers as the leader of the group. Truth be told, you never will. Therefore, turn up the heat by inviting everyone to ask their big, hairy questions. Seek out the answers in scripture together, and wrestle through the tough issues of life, doubt, and sin together. In between gatherings, use whatever tools and technology you can to keep your communication going, and enjoy the (messy) goodness that comes with real, authentic relationships like those found in the small batch.

CONNECTING WITH YOUR WHOLE SELF

Jesus was asked once what the most important command for God's children to obey was, and He answered by quoting ancient Jewish scriptures found in the Old Testament, "The most important one...is this: 'Hear O Israel, the Lord our God, the Lord is one. Love the Lord your God with all your heart and with all your soul and with all your mind, and with all your strength.' The second is this: 'Love your neighbor as yourself.' There is no commandment greater than these." (Mark 12:29-31)

Loving God in all these ways requires you to also love yourself and the people around you in the same manner. How can we love God with our entire being when we neglect any one significant part of our own humanity? Let's remember God made us in His own image, and therefore every part of us is intentional, beautiful and important, including everything Jesus mentioned above: our emotions, our spirit, our intellect, and our body. Each of these elemental pieces of ourselves should be considered along the discipleship journey. No single part of you can be excluded if you are going to become the most life-filled person God designed you to be. Therefore, encourage one another's health and wellness emotionally, spiritually, mentally, and physically.

You are a complex and wonderful creation, so think about growing your whole self as you journey with Jesus in order to enjoy Him and your human experience more fully. For example:

- Press pause regularly throughout the day to move and stretch.
- Step outside, and take some full, deep breaths. Your lungs were made for this.
- Go for a walk, jog or hike, or do something that gets your blood pumping.
- Eat food you not only enjoy but that nourishes your body.
- Venture out to learn something that lights your fire intellectually or fascinates you.
- Find a good counselor for mental health whenever needed.
- Explore the rich depth of your own human emotions, seeking to understand and use them more beneficially in your interactions with others. (For starters, I'd suggest reading *Emotional Intelligence 2.0* by Jean Greaves and Travis Bradberry[5].)
- Try your hand at a hobby that calls upon your creative side.

Try choosing just one of these activities to focus on each week, whichever feels most life-giving at the time. Think about how you can thank and enjoy God while you are experiencing all these things, and cheer along your small batch sisters in all these same ways. When you gather together, be intentional about creating experiences which are not only challenging, but also creative, engaging, and refreshing. As you seek to create meaningful conversations within your small batch, consider using the E.M.P.A.T.H.Y. technique. Harvard psychiatrist, Helen Riess, identified seven empathy traits that create strong interpersonal connections using neurobiology research[6]. They are as follows, and I paraphrase:

- **E: Eye contact** - look at one another, gather face-to-face whenever possible.
- **M: Muscles for facial expression** - mimic one another's sentiments, but remember that real smiles are distinguishable from fake ones.
- **P: Posture** - sit up tall and at eye level, face one another, lean in while you listen.
- **A: Affect -**pay attention to each other's emotional state.
- **T: Tone of voice -** match others' volume and pace, use soothing tones to spark compassionate conversations.
- **H: Hearing the whole person -** listen without interrupting, suspend judgment when emotions are running high.
- **Y: Your response -** be intentional with how you respond to others, emotions are contagious.

In essence, remain emotionally present wherever your feet touch the ground. Be where your feet are, and offer your whole self to the experience and people before you. Consider your humanity more deeply so you can live and worship more fully.

LISTENING WITH OTHERS IN MIND

So faith comes from hearing, and hearing through the word of Christ.

Romans 10:17 (ESV)

As I shared previously in this book, prior to coming to faith in Jesus Christ, I had a basic idea about who God was. I heard His Word read aloud on multiple occasions, but honestly it seemed foolish to me (1 Cor. 1:18). My ears were dull. Scripture went in one ear and out the other. Has this ever happened to you? Quoting the Old Testament, Jesus once spoke about the highly religious people of his day, "Though seeing, they do not see; though hearing, they do not hear or understand" (Matt. 13:13), and, "You will be ever hearing but never understanding; you will be ever seeing but never perceiving. For this people's heart has become calloused; they hardly hear with their ears, and they have closed their eyes. Otherwise, they might see with their eyes, hear with their ears, understand with their hearts and turn, and I would heal them" (Matt. 13:14-15). What a startling statement! This should capture our attention. For the faithful, those of us whose hearts have been softened by the gospel of Jesus Christ, this verse points out our opportunity to hear from God and be changed. We can either become better expressions of ourselves because of the working of his Word in our heart, or we can remain sick in our sin.

Parables are simple stories about common, everyday items intended to illustrate deeper spiritual truths. I've heard it said that a parable is like a handle Jesus puts into our hands to help us pick up a truth and take it home with us. During His earthly ministry, Jesus often conveyed spiritual concepts in parables to the crowds who gathered to hear Him teach, which He later explained to his disciples in greater depth in order to help them understand the deeper meaning of the stories. Let's take a look at one of the most widely known parables of Jesus, the Parable of the Sower found in Matthew 13. While this is referred to as the Parable of the Sower, the main subject of the story is, in fact, the *soil* onto which the sower flings his seeds. It's the soil that contains the greater truth Jesus wants us to grab hold of and carry home with us. Not surprisingly, it's about our hearing.

> *Then he told them many things in parables, saying: "A farmer went out to sow his seed. As he was scattering the seed, some fell along the path, and the birds came and ate it up. Some fell on rocky places, where it did not have much soil. It sprang up quickly, because the soil was shallow. But when the sun came up, the plants were scorched, and they withered because they had no root. Other seed fell among thorns, which grew up and choked the plants. Still other seed fell on good soil, where it produced a crop—a hundred, sixty or thirty times what was sown. Whoever has ears, let them hear."*

Matt. 13:3-9

THE SOIL OF OUR HEARTS

What people hear when confronted with God's word is determined by the spiritual sensitivity of their heart. Luke 8:11 instructs that the "seed" is the Word of God, and Matthew 13:19 explains that the "soil" represents our heart. In this parable, we see four different types of soil, and the seed penetrates each one differently. The first type of soil Jesus describes as roadside soil found along the farmer's path, hardened from all the farmer's walking back and forth. The seed never makes it below the surface of the dirt and is quickly snatched up by birds. Jesus explains when anyone in this condition hears the message about the kingdom of God and doesn't understand it, the evil one comes along and snatches away what was sown in her heart. This person may be self-absorbed or content with the comforts of life, they may feel they've heard it all before, or perhaps they are angry or indifferent toward the things of God. Either way, she doesn't receive the truth of God's message because of the hardness of her heart.

The second type of soil is shallow soil atop a hard layer of rock. The seed that falls here springs up with a quick show of life, but because there is no root, the growing plants are easily scorched in the heat of the sun and die. Jesus describes the person like this as one who hears and receives the word of God with joy, but her enthusiasm lasts only a short time until trouble or persecution comes along. Then she quickly falls away. This person's heart has competing loyalties and lacks the depth of faith required to persevere in the face of criticism or hardship. Simply put, she isn't able to give her whole heart and whole self in response to God's Word.

The third type of soil mentioned in this parable is repressive soil, where the life that grows up from the seed is choked out by thorns. This listener hears and receives the Word of God, but the worries of life and the false allure of wealth or worldly indulgence monopolize this person's time, attention, and resources, until there is no room left for faith and obedience to bloom. A personal idol or sinful behavior takes the throne in this person's life and prevents uninhibited connection with God. Due to distraction, indifference, competing allegiances, or sin, our hearts can fall into these first three categories at any time, though most of us are quick to assume we fit into the final category of soils - good soil.

The fourth type of soil Jesus describes is reproductive soil, and it produces a crop many times greater than what was sown. A woman whose heart is represented by fertile soil hears the Word of God and understands it. She doesn't resist God's prompting in her life and is in full cooperation with the King. Furthermore, there is a harvest that follows her, as a handful of little seeds one day yields an unimaginable abundance of life. As followers of Christ, this is the spiritual condition we long for. It's this kind of receptive and obedient listening to the Word of God that feeds us individually and blesses the other people in our lives, much like the community surrounding a farmer's field.

Rocky Soil

• Hardened, not receptive

Shallow Soil

• Quickly excited, but turns back to old ways when difficulty arises

Thorny Soil

• Distracted by sinful habits, comforts, and worldly or self-centered cares

Good Soil

• Prepared, receptive, obedient, and reproductive

Does the Word of God sink down deep within your heart when you read or hear it? Does it change you? Are you moved to action and ever increasing Christ-likeness? Do you share His truth with others? Is your heart good soil? Let's be realistic, each of us is probably bouncing between all four types of heart soil even on our best days: sometimes disinterested, often distracted, maybe even entangled. But prayerfully, yours can be the kind of heart where God can plant His beautiful seed of purpose and truth and nourish it to harvest. If that's not where you are today, feel free to put this book down. Or better yet, pass it along to someone you know who needs it. In all likelihood, you won't keep running with this unless God is fueling your heart to do so. However, if this sounds like you and something inside of you is stirring to join Jesus and figure the rest of this thing out, then I urge you to keep reading.

CHECK THE SOIL

As you search for disciples of your own over the years, check the soil. Naturally, a potential disciple won't understand all the discipleship journey entails until it plays out awhile, and she can't grasp the joy of a daily connection with God until she's experienced one. We can't hunger for what we haven't yet tasted, but watch for her openness to God and her obedience to His prompting. Meanwhile, as you love on people and talk about God, fling the "seed" of the gospel just like the farmer did, indiscriminately and wholesale-style. Open the front door of your life to all those who respond. Over time, if you sense someone pressing in for more of what God is doing in your life, if she remains faithful and willing to work at it, then you've found good soil. Plant there.

Consider a flower. It blooms up and out, springing with life from the ground below. The strategy of Jesus Christ for you who follow in His footsteps is to be just like that flower, always keeping the beauty of the Word of God in the forefront of your mind, love abounding in your heart and hands. His love builds deep within us, and it blooms upward and outward into the world.

Above all, I must have flowers, always, and always.[7]

Claude Monet

MEET JENN

When I graduated college and moved to the mountains to manage races and events for a ski resort, I called my good friend Jenn to see what she had lined up for work. With nothing planned, she packed her bags and moved into the resort's employee housing with me. She was hired as a ski lift operator, a "liftie" as they're known, and we became roomies. Jenn journeyed with me during my time of spiritual searching as well as during my season of courtship with this cute Southern boy who eventually became my husband. Truthfully, she can tell stories about me I'd much prefer to forget.

The ski season came and went as quickly as a snowstorm, and our lives took us different directions for a while. After a decade or so, we reconnected over lunch and caught up on all of life's twists and turns through marriage, children, work, and faith. I remember her saying something like, "Okay, Tracy, I've gotta be honest. Something is beautifully different about you, and I need to hear more about it." Jenn pressed in to know more, and I flung some seed. She listened as I shared about all God had been doing in our lives, and she reminded me how dissimilar I sounded from when we'd lived together. I invited her to join the group of women meeting at our house each week, and she took me up on the offer. Later Jenn confessed to me how when she left our house after those first few weeks, she called her friend Dianna on the way home and admitted to her she honestly wasn't sure what she'd gotten herself into. She told Dianna how we memorized scripture, studied the Bible, prayed together, and got deep into the nitty-gritty of one another's lives. She explained how she really loved me as a friend. After all, our friendship was at the in-one-another's-wedding-party level, so she'd keep coming for two or three more weeks but probably would stop coming over after that. Aside from being a wonderful wife and mom, Jenn was a kick-butt career woman, and her passion for public relations and marketing encompassed most of her time and energy, so she was busy. I never knew of the sidebar conversation going on with Dianna.

Jenn had always believed in Jesus and regularly attended church with her family growing up, but she had missed out on a personal, daily connection with Him and on understanding the incredible purpose God has for her life. It thrills me to say after a year of deepening her faith through discipleship, Jenn shared with me, "Tracy, I just want you to know, God has flipped my life upside down. I'd quit my job to do this forever." The beautiful thing is, she didn't have to.

Jenn's heart was good soil, and God's love grew up and out from her life, spilling over into those conversations with Dianna. Dianna naturally became Jenn's first disciple, and other women jumped on board within just a few months to learn more about Jesus from both of them, from the board room to their neighborhoods and everywhere in between. God turned my college pal and roomie into a lifelong friend and partner in ministry, with a garden of faith in full bloom in her life. The Lord writes the most dazzling stories!

SHARING IS CARING

I notice small batch things everywhere I go these days. Maybe it's similar to the phenomenon that happens when you get a new car, and all of a sudden you notice how many matching cars there are out on the road. Somehow you never saw them, but now you can't *not* see them. For me, it's all things "small batch." One day recently, I noticed a small batch chocolate bar in the checkout lane at the local market, and I just had to buy it. How could I *not* buy a chocolate bar with "small batch" on the wrapper? I handed it to the grocer, and she added it to my bag. When I got home, I ate a small piece of this delicious, dark and stormy chocolate bar, and I decided to save the rest to enjoy for a few more days, one square at a time. I tucked it above the stove in one of the top cabinets where no one would look. Jon looked. And that night, while I was fast asleep, my night-owl husband enjoyed the rest of my small batch chocolate bar with a nice, cold glass of milk.

I suppose a really great treat is even better when shared with someone you love. Albert Einstein once said, "Only a life lived for others is a life worthwhile."[8] To that end, just like my chocolate bar, the presence of the Word of God in your life is not intended for your consumption alone. You are responsible to steward the truth God entrusts to you even beyond yourself. Sharing is caring. God means for each of us to hear and understand it, to consider and obey it, to be changed by it, and ultimately to share it with others.

Encourage one another and build each other up.

1 Thessalonians 5:11

THE POWER OF THE SEED

God still speaks to us today. He does so in many ways, but the primary means through which He communicates with us is through the Bible. It is His message, His voice, a love letter written to you and me, His beloved. And found within its rich pages is a treasure of truth and life. A Judean date palm seed about 2,000 years old, nicknamed Methuselah, was recovered in 1973 from excavations at Masada, a historic mountainside fortress in Israel near the Dead Sea where the Jewish people clashed against the Romans after a two-year siege in AD 73. It was germinated in 2005 by botanical archaeologists, demonstrating to the world the enduring germination power of a seed.[9] Another seed, a Sacred Lotus seed recovered from a dry lakebed in northeast China in 1995, also reproduced and was carbon-14 dated to be 1,350 years old.[10] What life and power resided inside those seeds all those years!

The "seed" of the Word of God has germinating, chain-breaking, life-giving power greater even than these examples. But be warned, hearing the Word of God over and over and not responding to it leads to hardened soil. The farmer's footsteps eventually press the dirt down enough that it becomes so hard the seed won't break through the surface anymore. If the soil of your heart is hard, dry, and calloused from years of ignoring God's call, it's possible you just won't hear what He's saying anymore. Please don't do this. I plead with you to open your ears! Listen and be changed by the love letter that was written to bring your heart back to life.

On the other hand, when God's Word is carefully planted in the good soil of a divinely prepared heart, a harvest beyond your wildest imagination will grow. What will you do with the truth you've already heard and will continue to hear from the Lord? Will you receive and obey it? Will you share it with others? Might you intentionally invest that truth by making disciples of others? Inside-out, others-focused living is God's desire for our lives. It's exactly how Jesus lived, giving of Himself to the very limit even unto death, to enable you and me to enjoy a loving relationship with God forever. Let God set you free from the tyranny of a self-centered life. Be sure to listen with others in mind. Your hearing is not meant for you alone.

Then you will know the truth, and the truth will set you free.

John 8:32

KEY CONCEPTS

- When seeking someone to disciple, look for all the people around you who know the least about Jesus *and* those who are hungriest for God and for greater purpose for their lives.
- Disciples are teachable, available, committed, and others-oriented (T.A.C.O.).
- Be thoughtful and protective about the purpose of your small batch gatherings. Create cultural norms where everyone feels safe, use empathy to connect, and don't avoid difficult conversations or questions that arise.
- True hearing involves listening with an open mind and a willingness to be changed by what you've heard. When it comes to the Word of God, this is what it means to have a heart with "good soil."
- You are responsible to steward the truth God entrusts to you beyond yourself.

DISCUSSION QUESTIONS

1. How do the T.A.C.O. characteristics of a disciple resonate with you? Explain.
2. Have you participated in or hosted personal gatherings that incorporated a clear purpose, meaningful cultural norms, or included an element of "heat"? Describe your experience.
3. Do you ever have difficulty focusing on what others

are saying to you in conversation? Why or why
not? How might using empathy help you connect
more deeply with others?

4. Reread the parable of the soils in Matthew 13:3-9.
Which obstacle most often gets in your way of
hearing or obeying God: distraction, indifference,
competing allegiances, or sin?

5. Is it possible to have fertile soil in some areas of
your heart and not in others when responding to
the Word of God? Explain.

6. In what ways might you share God's Word and His
love more intentionally with others?

part two

two

Foundations of Discipleship

chapter three

Embracing Your
greater purpose

God wants more for you than you do. [1]

Jon Bloom

Peter is a widely beloved character in the Bible. People identify with him for multiple reasons, not the least of which is his ongoing wrestling match of saint-and-sinner-like characteristics. For many of us, Peter's story is like looking in a full length mirror. Interestingly, in reading about the moment he met Jesus face-to-face, we catch a glimpse of the miraculous way God loves *us* just as we are and yet also calls us to be so much more with His help. Undoubtedly, Peter could have never imagined God's mighty plan for his life. Isn't that just the way God works in our lives even now? He continues to make beauty from ashes and accomplishes incredible things while using seemingly impossible material.

Let's take a look in scripture when Jesus calls Peter to follow Him (John 1:42). Remember before he met Jesus, Peter was first known as Simon. First, Simon was brought to Jesus by his brother Andrew. Then, Jesus addressed him, saying, "You are Simon son of John. You will be called Cephas," an Aramaic name which when translated into the Greek language of the day meant Peter, or "rock." It was a quick exchange, but a significant one. Jesus looked into the eyes of Simon and saw him as he really was, but He also saw more in him. He beheld Peter.

What does Jesus see when He looks at you and me? I'll start. If you ask those I work with, they might describe me as a confident, joyful, caring, and energetic woman. While that's true most of the time, those I personally live with might layer in additional shades of color. I'm also restless, overly sensitive, bossy, and prideful at times. All-in-all, this probably represents a more complete picture. Jesus sees all of this in me and infinitely much more. He perceives my innermost thoughts and my best-laid plans. As if having spiritual X-ray vision, there is nothing Jesus doesn't know about me. Furthermore, He adds an eternal perspective that outweighs my own ability to see and know myself. You see (pun intended), Jesus understands the whole picture of me, just as I am.

Jesus saw Simon just as he was, too: a rash, cursing, quick-tempered, and impulsive fisherman. Simon was a hot mess, not to mention quite the opposite of his brother Andrew, the more steady and reliable of the two. As a matter of fact, three of the five times we hear about Andrew in the Bible, he was bringing someone else to Jesus. Surely Jesus would call *him* the rock instead of Simon, right? Remarkably, though, that's not at all what happened.

SPIRITUAL BIFOCALS

I've worn eyeglasses or contacts since I was twelve years

old. My vision is honestly pretty ghastly without them. A few years ago, I upgraded my frames to a chunky pair of Juicy Couture leopard print specs. They're pretty cute, but there's one problem. I also like wearing my contacts, especially when I'm feeling sporty and want to go for a run, because everyone who has worn glasses while exercising knows that sweating in glasses is the worst. My dilemma is people tell me they think something's missing when I don't wear my glasses. I'm guessing my look seems off somehow when there's a lack of leopard. What's a girl to do?

In 1784, Ben Franklin penned his feelings of frustration about his eyeglasses in a handwritten letter to a friend.[2] An age-old dilemma, Franklin grew tired of switching back and forth from one pair of eyeglasses for reading to another pair of nearsighted spectacles. Crafting together one-half of a convex lens and one-half of a concave lens, he created the first pair of bifocals. What any bifocal-wearer knows, though, is that learning to use both lenses in concert is no easy task. Franklin surely experienced the same dizziness and headaches during his first attempts at wearing "double spectacles" as anyone today. However, once the novelty wears off, such specs open up a whole new world of sight to their users, offering both up-close and far off vision simultaneously.

Looking back at our short text in John 1:42, the actual word used to describe what Jesus did when He "looked at" Simon is important. In the original Greek in which these words were recorded, this word we translate "looked at" is *emblepo*. It means to behold, to look upon, to observe fixedly, to look at with the mind, or to discern clearly.[3] If you examine and combine the two root words of *emblepo*, *en* and *blepo*, you also garner "to see into." It's as if Jesus could see right into Simon to the very core. If we imagine Jesus wearing spiritual bifocals, then this would be the up close, lower lens.

Time to bring it home and circle back to the other part of the "you and me" question. How does Jesus behold you?

Allow your mind to wander a few moments and be honest with yourself. How might you answer that question? What about those who know you best? What more does Jesus see that maybe even you or your dearest loved ones do not? The reality is He sees every bit of you too. You're not invisible to God. Meanwhile, He sees right through the persona you project to show the world how you have it all together. And honestly, He loves every part of you. He doesn't need you to fix or cover up anything to come to Him, just like Simon, because He has plans to rejoice over and redeem every part of your story. You are seen, friend. You're known, forgiven, and treasured all at once.

"You are Simon," Jesus said. Although beholding His new friend in all his Simon-ness, Jesus graciously dared to still call Peter a "rock," and Simon Peter's redemption story began. What hope! Bifocals have two lenses, and here Jesus used the upper lens to look ahead into the future. Like double vision, Jesus was able to discern Peter as he was but also as he *could* be. He saw the man God's grace could make out of him, and the two people were so different it warranted giving Simon a different name.

We actually see name changes multiple times in scripture. Think of Jacob, a liar and a cheat, who after spiritually and physically wrestling with God was renamed Israel and became father to the nation of God's people representing the same name. Or Saul, the horrible persecutor of early Christians who later became Paul through God's gracious and redeeming power, a humble and wildly impactful Christ-follower. Consider Abraham and Sarah, once Abram and Sarai, who grew in faith by obediently waiting many years for the fulfillment of God's promise to them to have children. Levi, the swindling tax collector, became Matthew, the apostle of Jesus and an evangelist. Let's not forget Jesus' more laughable designation of the brothers James and John as "Sons of Thunder." God has always been in the business of remaking lives.

SET FREE FROM SIN

It's once been said of the renowned sculptor, Michelangelo, that while he chipped away at a large unattractive block of rocky and raw marble, a friend approached and asked him what he was doing. He replied, "I saw an angel in the marble and carved until I set him free."[4] While you and I, and Simon Peter for that matter, are obviously not angels, Jesus is no less working in this same way at every moment to uncover and produce the possible person within. Don't forget, value is in the eye of the beholder. The value of something is determined by the price someone is willing to pay for it. Jesus paid the maximum price for you and me; therefore, our value — and ultimately our potential — is pretty impressive in His eyes. Maybe some of us need to hear this.

Others criticized Jesus for cultivating relationships with broken people like Simon Peter, critically calling him a "friend of sinners." However, Jesus saw the people as sheep without a shepherd and looked upon them with compassion and hope. He befriended sinners because they were just the sort of people who could see and feel their own need for God. They were humble. The Savior of the world brought salvation to all who would receive it, even those who seemed utterly beyond saving, and He thought they were worth it. Since this is still true today, how do sinners like you and me move from "Simon" to "Peter"? Jesus is the bridge, and like the earliest disciples we need a living, breathing relationship with Him. When we seek Jesus, He is willing to do the hard work of chiseling away at our fleshly selves until a clearer reflection of Him emerges (see Luke 13:6-9).

Let's quickly circle back to our sculpture illustration. Just around the corner from one of Michelangelo's greatest works of art, *David*, lie several of his non-finito sculptures. These statues, also known as the *Prisoners* (or *Slaves*), depict unfinished works of the artist's imagination, each one visibly straining to be set free from the weight of their surrounding stone as an illustration of the soul held captive by its flesh. It's a powerful picture of the struggle we all have against our fleshly, sinful nature. Paul said it this way, "I do not understand what I do. For what I want to do I do not do, but what I hate I do" (Rom. 7:15). Meanwhile, we must remember our God is a chain-breaker!

Chain-breaking was heavy on the heart and mind of Harriet Tubman as she bravely followed God's leadership in her life and delivered countless captives to the freedom all humans deserve. Born into slavery and scarred by abuse and hardship, Harriet Tubman herself escaped captivity in Maryland in 1849. She found her way to freedom in Pennsylvania via the Underground Railroad, and soon made it her mission to continue traveling this perilous path so others might also taste freedom.[5] Known as the "Moses of her people,"[6] Tubman made 19 trips between 1850 and 1860 as a "conductor" along the Underground Railroad, helping more than 300 enslaved people make the journey from Southern slave territories in the US to the free Northern territories. A follower of Jesus, Tubman's motto was "I can't die but once."[7] Therefore, with her eyes fixed on the eternal life to come, she lived the earthly one fully and allowed God to accomplish mighty Kingdom work both in and through her.

Jesus is the one and only Way (John 14:6) for you to be set free from the chains of sin that weigh you down. The shackles which held you down and back in the past don't have a grip on your future. In order to step into the life God designed for you, it's your responsibility to turn from your former way of living life on your own and to believe in Jesus Christ with your entire being. Abandon life on your own terms and embrace God's way of life, which is exceedingly full and brings the promise of forever with Him. Jesus said, "The thief comes only to steal and kill and destroy; I have come that they may have life, and have it to the full," (John 10:10). As Simon does, you drop your fishing net, take up your cross, and follow Jesus. It's not always going to be easy, but there is no Plan B.

But, wait. Don't we all have personal goals and aspirations already in place for our own lives? Of course we do, but let's not overlook one important and relevant detail in Simon Peter's story. After their first meeting, a period of time passed before Jesus actually called Simon to leave his fishing nets behind. He was first invited to simply get to know Jesus, watch Him work, listen, and consider His messages. We see in Mark's gospel it was actually some time later when Jesus returned to call Simon and his brother, Andrew, to follow him. They did so "at once," according to Mark's description, because after they knew Jesus, it was clear to these men He was worth devoting their lives to follow. They were more than ready to ditch the fishing nets in favor of following in the Messiah's footsteps. Does God also have a magnificent plan in store for our lives once we change course to follow Jesus? Without a doubt, yes! Let's take a look at a few things He is looking to accomplish in and through each one of us.

MATURITY

For starters, God desires to mature you and me as individual disciples. This goal is the same for every believer, to make us more like Himself. The first part of Romans 8:29 states it this way, "For those God foreknew he also predestined to be conformed to the likeness of his Son." God plans to make us more like Jesus. Similar to how Michaelangelo must have felt about his masterpiece, you and I are called God's *poiema* (Eph. 2:10), meaning His poem, handiwork, creation, masterpiece, and featured attraction. He is crazy about you! He has big plans for you. And this maturing process, this work of art, takes time. Truthfully, we won't ever arrive at a place of perfect spiritual maturity this side of heaven. I know I haven't.

Yet, we can become mature enough to invite others along on our journey. In the physical realm, reproduction requires a certain level of physical maturity. The same is true spiritually. As disciples, we grow in our walk with Jesus. Then, we help others a few steps behind to grow in their walk with Jesus, and we continue maturing right along with them.

Our kids recently asked me, with eyebrows raised and a long dramatic pause, if it was true I was born in the 1900s. Now, the truth was yes, I *was* born in the 1900s, but somehow the way this question was phrased made me sound a lot older than I am. I went on to explain the 1900s represented an entire century, and I was born later in that time period. My explanation was lost, though, amidst their gasps of horror and awe. According to my kids' perspectives, this fact dated me right up there with Cleopatra. It's fine, though. I'm fine. Everything's fine. What's in a number anyhow? Whatever my birth year and age, I'm still a spring chicken on the inside and always will be. Aren't we all? In reality, none of us has yet arrived at the finish line of life, so we're all simply continuing on a journey of maturing.

Pulling back into our story of Simon Peter's life one final time, a fascinating progression unfolded as Jesus matured and developed him. He first acted solely out of his Simon nature, but later he behaved more and more like Peter. We walk this same journey. You and I begin like babies in Christ, and over the course of our lives as Christians, we grow stronger and more consistent in our love affair with Him. Jesus becomes our first love and our nearest companion. His Word comes alive to us, sharpening and satisfying our hearts and minds. People might even start to notice how we walk, talk and *smell* more Christ. Smell, really? Yes, smell. As the Bible puts it, we are the fragrance of Christ.

But thanks be to God, who always leads us as captives in Christ's triumphal procession and uses us to spread the aroma of the knowledge of him everywhere. For we are to God the pleasing aroma of Christ among those who are being saved and those who are perishing. To the one we are an aroma that brings death; to the other, an aroma that brings life...

2 Cor 2:14-16

MISSION

Secondly, God plans to give each of us a mission in His gospel movement. Part of Peter's purpose in life was to become a mighty preacher, who on the Day of Pentecost (found in Acts 2) publicly declared the gospel and led *three thousand* people to faith in Jesus Christ! He became one of the two foremost leaders of the Apostles, those sent out into the world by Jesus, and the early church. Peter also wrote the two books found in our New Testament reflecting his name. And this is the guy who once flew off the handle in anger on a regular basis, smelled like fish, spoke like a sailor, and even denied Christ just before the cross!

I'd be remiss if I didn't also mention how God used Paul in a surprising way, too. Paul described himself as "circumcised on the eighth day, of the people of Israel, of the tribe of Benjamin, a Hebrew of Hebrews; in regard to the law, a Pharisee; as for zeal, persecuting the church; as for righteousness based on the law, faultless" (Phil. 3:4-6). What a resume! After an encounter with Jesus that literally stopped him in his murderous tracks (Acts 9:1-22), God used *this* man to bring the good news of the gospel, not to his former group of religious aristocrats though none were more qualified for that job, but rather to the non-religious Gentile people Paul once looked down upon (Eph. 4:12). And God's completed mission through Paul was precisely how you and I found a seat at God's table of grace. God's plans are *far* better than ours. Just like Peter and Paul, we couldn't guess them if we tried.

When I began my own discipleship adventure in 2010, I was ready to say yes to the first mission trip opportunity that presented itself overseas. It wouldn't take much to convince someone with a lifelong case of wanderlust to sign up for an international adventure with Jesus, and so I did. After all, God had a place for me in His gospel mission! Of all possible desti-nations, the trip I signed up for was going back to Peru, where I'd said no to God all those years ago. It was finally my chance to return to the place that had become such a special part of my redemption story carrying the good news of the gospel. Unfortunately, my best laid plans didn't play out like I'd expected.

Everything about *my* plan seemed perfect. My boys were big enough to be without me for a week or so. Jon was able to take off work to stay home with them and help them feel a part of things from this side of the world. The team going on this trip was the absolute best. And, c'mon, it was Peru! It was all settled, or so I thought.

Early one morning, just weeks out from the big trip, Jon and I were hacking our way through a high-intensity workout program, when I nearly passed out on the floor. What on earth was wrong? I couldn't possibly imagine, that is, until a little blue stick confirmed it. We were expecting our third child! And no, I didn't get to go on that trip, but another one even-tually came, and another, and another. In the meantime, God gave Jon and I the greatest blessing we didn't even know to ask for. *Yes*, He still had a mission for me in His gospel movement, both at home and abroad. *And*, His plans were far better than mine. They always are.

We are far too easily pleased.[8]

C.S. Lewis

MULTIPLICATION

Finally, God has another objective in mind for us, to give us a personal ministry of multiplication. Peter multiplied the value of his own faith and life by pouring himself into the life of John Mark, his disciple. As a matter of fact, when John Mark later transcribed all that his discipler taught him, it was Peter's action-oriented demeanor that caused Mark's gospel account to be the most fast-paced, action-oriented presentation of the life of Jesus in the Bible. Apparently, even Peter's tempo rubbed off on his protégé over time. Peter referred to John Mark as "Mark, my son" in his own writings (1 Pet. 5:13), and we surmise the closeness of their relationship when Peter escaped from prison and immediately sought refuge in John Mark's mother's house, where the church people had gathered to pray for him. What a compelling picture of the personal impact of discipleship! As a young believer, John Mark sat at the feet of Peter, an older and wiser man who knew and loved Jesus. He listened intently, took notes, and repeated everything that God, through his discipler, entrusted to him. And through the works of God in Mark's life, the truths of Jesus have been multiplied to the present day beyond measure.

...and what you have heard from me in the presence of many witnesses entrust to faithful men, who will be able to teach others also.

2 Timothy 2:2 (ESV)

Before I met Jesus, I was once told in a bar that my "aura" was really powerful. Is that what happens when two yogis walk into a bar? I'm still not sure. Though I can't vouch for my aura, I can say with confidence that my spiritual maturity at that time was next to nil. Today, because of the influence of Christ in my life through discipleship, I've come a long way. I'm still on the journey, but I'm standing on the Rock. I know Jesus, and I've seen His faithfulness enough times in my life that my faith has taken root. I'm all-in on the small batch, mission accepted. And I've already lost count of the lives that our Great God has impacted *through* the women He's placed in my small batch circles. He's doing it, y'all! He's using me and others like me, cracks and all. I don't know why that should be surprising. It's been His plan from the very beginning.

God is looking to accomplish maturity, mission, and multiplication in your life, as well. Your sins and struggles don't have to get in the way of God's work in and through you. He sees you. He knows you and has chosen you. God values every part of you and your life story, and He can use it all for His glory. Get ready! There is more to God's plan for your life than you have yet imagined.

YOUR IDENTITY IN CHRIST

How do you define yourself today? Is your identity shaped by your past mistakes or successes? Your singleness or your marriage? Your children's accolades or challenges, or the struggle to conceive children at all? Maybe your definition of self is wrapped up in the condition of your home, your physique, or your career. The truth is none of these define who you are or what your future might hold. Your true and lasting identity is found in who God says you are and what He has planned for you. He created you, after all, and is the Author of your life story. As T. S. Eliot offers, "Every moment is a fresh beginning."[9] With every breath you take, with every sunrise that shines into the darkness, God is making all things new.

> *Therefore, if anyone is in Christ, he is a new creation; the old has gone, the new has come!*
>
>   2 Corinthians 5:17 (ESV)

Scripture illuminates the theme of "newness" brightly from its pages. We are told those who trust in Christ receive a *new* heart, a *new* spirit, and a *new* life. They are under a *new* covenant with God. There is a *new* man, a *new* birth, and even in the days ahead, a *new* Jerusalem. So I'd like to explore the answer to this question: What's *new* for a Christian?

After working through the first part of this book, we know God speaks, and that what He says to you and me is intended not only for us, but also for those around us. We also know God has much, much bigger purposes in mind for our lives as Christians than we can imagine. But does anything actually change about us once we rest all of our hopes in Jesus? Are we *really* any different than we were before believing? Now we're going to explore the three "P's" you receive as a result of choosing life with Christ: your new position, possession, and product.

NEW POSITION: IN CHRIST

I am the true vine, and my Father is the gardener. He cuts off

every branch in me that bears no fruit, while every branch
that does bear fruit he prunes so that it will be even more
fruitful. You are already clean because of the word I have
spoken to you. Remain in me, as I also remain in you. No
branch can bear fruit by itself; it must remain in the vine.
Neither can you bear fruit unless you remain in me.
I am the vine; you are the branches. If you remain in me and I
in you, you will bear much fruit; apart from me you can
do nothing. If you do not remain in me, you are like a
branch that is thrown away and withers; such branches are
picked up, thrown into the fire and burned. If you remain
in me and my words remain in you, ask whatever you
wish, and it will be done for you. This is to my Father's
glory, that you bear much fruit, showing yourselves to be
my disciples.
As the Father has loved me, so have I loved you. Now remain in
my love. If you keep my commands, you will remain in my
love, just as I have kept my Father's commands and remain
in his love. I have told you this so that my joy may be in you
and that your joy may be complete.

John 15:1-11

In one of the last lessons Jesus teaches His disciples before
His death on the cross, He paints this beautiful picture of the
vine and the branches. Jesus is the vine, and we are the
branches. Many years ago, I traveled by train across a vast
European countryside. I gazed for long hours out the windows
without blinking. I marveled at the sun-kissed beauty of that
scene. Mile upon mile, olive groves covered the terrain with
their earthy greens and deep shades of gray and brown. And
those vineyards! Grapevines stood rooted in the earth and
seemed confident from centuries of cultivation. The vines
dripped with grapes ripe for the harvest, and I imagined tables
in nearby villages pregnant with romantic stories and laughter,

a crusty loaf of bread, a dish of oil and herbs, and glasses fit for the fruit of the vine.

A meal shared with loved ones over a rustic kitchen table of course, while tasty, is really a matter of relationship. The Christian life, too, is not merely one of religion and ritual, but rather a deep, abiding, and soul-satisfying relationship. Isn't this what we are all searching for? To be known, enjoyed, and loved? It's as if our hearts were made from the very beginning with some sort of crater inside, a hole that absolutely *must* be filled, and we search in every direction for something or someone who can do it. Yet, as we all eventually learn, nothing can fill this void besides the One by whom and for whom this space inside us was fashioned. Our longings can never be satisfied by the things of this world, whether drugs or alcohol, sex, busyness, work, social media likes, retail therapy, fitness, etc. They all turn up empty and dull in the end, leaving us alone, sad, and hurting. But Jesus. Oh, friend! Like the missing piece to the puzzle, Jesus alone can fill the chasm of our longing. Our loving Savior never disappoints. His friendship never fades, His company never departs, and His treasure never rusts. Jesus is called the Living Water, and I promise you the well never runs dry. Jesus' very life and presence is what's new and different about the Christian life. To experience this, the branches must stay rooted in the vine. You must stay connected to Jesus.

Have you ever received a promotion at work or landed a new gig? What about moving into a new home or to a new town? So much excitement comes with those new positions, both professional and physical ones. Did you know, as a believer, you have a new position too? Six times in just seven verses within John chapter 15, Jesus says "in Me." Paul uses the phrase "in Christ" 164 times throughout his New Testament letters. Our new position as Christians is therefore *in Christ*. In order to fully understand this, though, it might be helpful to compare our old position with our new one.

For as in Adam all die, so in Christ all will be made alive.

1 Corinthians 15:22

Therefore, there is now no condemnation for those who are in Christ Jesus, for the law of the Spirit of life set me free from the law of sin and death.

Romans 8:1-2

Although we all start out positionally in Adam, headed hopelessly toward sin and death, everyone who is positioned through faith in Christ has already been made into a new creation, spiritually justified and headed toward life and freedom with God forever. Can I get an amen? I once heard a story about an African American man who lived in Missouri back before the Emancipation Proclamation and the freeing of American slaves. This man, a slave hopelessly bound to his earthly master, lived on a peninsula that jutted out into the Mississippi River. One night, he went to sleep in his cabin on the river, just as every night before. The neighboring river rose over the banks that night and the peninsula flooded, breaking off from the mainland and becoming a river isle. Remarkably, the law stated that any land mass not connected to Missouri was officially part of the state of Illinois…the *free* state of Illinois! This man went to sleep that night a slave, and he awoke a free man. What was the difference? Simply his position. Given he would likely spend the rest of his life adjusting to his new reality and responsibility as a free man, we will do the very same thing adjusting to ours. Sin and death have held us all captive and chained down through fear, pain, and loneliness. But know this: if you love and follow Jesus, you have been set free. You are no longer *in Adam*, hopelessly bound by your sins and failures, but you are *in Christ*, a citizen of Heaven.

NEW POSSESSION: CHRIST IN YOU

Your new position also brings with it a new possession, and that is "Christ in you." In John 15:4 Jesus says he will "remain in you" when you abide in him. In John 1:12, we are told we are made children of God when we "receive" Jesus. Colossians 1:27 calls Jesus "Christ in you, the hope of glory." In Galatians 2:20, Paul says that having been crucified with Christ, Christ "lives in" the believer. And finally, in 1 John 5:12 we read the person who "has" the Son has life. So Christ Jesus is *in* us, filling that holy chasm as only He can, and we are *in* Him. There is really no earthly illustration that can completely capture this concept, and I'm not sure our fantastic, yet limited, minds can comprehend something as spectacular and other-worldly as this. It helps me, though, to picture a sponge drenched in water. The sponge is indeed in the water, but the water is also in the sponge. If you grab a hot coal out of the fireplace, you'll find that while the coal was in the fire, so too the fire is in the coal. Now obviously this doesn't come close to capturing the spiritual reality that the King of the universe is living inside the believer while he or she walks and talks and goes about living. Obviously, this is wildly profound. According to God's own Word, though, I have the Person who scripture says created all things and who holds all things together literally living through His Spirit inside me. If this is true (and it is), isn't this then, by far, the most significant thing about my life? Shouldn't this reality change absolutely everything?

A question comes to mind for me, and maybe also for you, about whether Jesus intends then to replace us as He moves in. John says, "He must become greater; I must become less" (John 3:30). While this is true of our ever increasing Christlikeness, let's not forget our God made each one of us uniquely, intentionally, and He calls us "very good" (Gen.

1:31). He is proud of who He made you to be. Your personality and life story is by design the very thing Jesus will use to fully display His goodness to a world that is desperate to see Him. Therefore, you are a living vessel intended to contain His presence as you go about your way. There needs to be constant interaction between you and Jesus, an ongoing communion of sorts that is, in all honesty, a consistent juxtaposition of sweet and messy. And this sweet, messy relationship is the only way to have real fulfillment in life. You are not meant to live this life alone. The one and only Person who has ever been able to perfectly live the Christian life is desiring to do in each one of us what we could never do on our own.

It's true, God saves us to restore and enjoy the relationship He intended to have with us all along; but, if that were His only purpose in our salvation, then I have to believe that He would have already swooped us up to heaven to be with Him. He didn't, though. There are still many of us believers running around on this planet, which has to mean His purposes continue to unfold through His people. Jesus doesn't save us merely to get us out of earth and into Heaven, but also to get Himself out of Heaven and onto earth again. His presence is now multiplied beyond even just one earthly body. How marvelous! What an ingenious plan! God's heart is for others, too, and our antennae should go up realizing everywhere we go, the Spirit of Christ is within us waiting to be revealed to all those who hunger and thirst for Him. Our neighbors are like sheep without a shepherd, as each of us once were, seeking something to fill the holy vacuum in their hearts, not knowing where to turn. The One who can save and satisfy them forever is *in you*.

NEW PRODUCT: FRUIT

A third mark of those whose identity is in Christ is a new product produced in our lives. In verse five of the vine and branches passage in John 15, Jesus says that a person who remains in Him, and therefore He in them, will bear fruit. As the branch connected to the grapevine bears grapes, so we bear "fruit unto God" (Rom. 7:4 King James Version). Additionally, in verses two and five of John 15, we see that our life's fruitfulness can vary from *no* fruit, to *some* or *more* fruit, or even *much* fruit. Are we talking kiwis, apples, and bananas? Obviously not. Rather, fruit in our lives is what results when the life of Christ overflows. Jesus said He has come to bring us an abundance of life (John 10:10), a surplus that will spill over from within us. Abiding in Christ, therefore, leads to an abundance for Christ. His life in us spills over unto others.

Many people, myself included, feel inspired by God's awesome work in the natural world. After all, nature reveals so much about its Creator. If we consider the grapevine, we'll notice that branches bearing grapes aren't struggling and straining to do so. Grapevines don't groan and grunt to squeeze out grapes. Fruit is a *natural* product of a healthy vine. Likewise, we don't need to struggle and strain to produce spiritual fruit in our lives. If our relationship with Jesus Christ is healthy and strong, then spiritual fruit is a given. It will come out naturally. Jesus says the one who remains in Him *will* bear fruit. His life in us *will* lead to fruit. Notice also the trees outside your window don't eat their own fruit. It's true, right? Apple trees don't consume apples. Banana trees don't eat their yellow bunches. Palm trees don't gobble up their coconuts. The fruit is produced for passersby. Fruit is for others. This is true of us spiritually, as well. Yes, the fruit Jesus says we will bear is both natural and meant for others, but precisely what *is* it?

Our new product, fruit, comes to bear in our lives in several shapes and forms. The Bible explains our character will become more Christ-like, and this takes the shape of the "fruit of the Spirit" found in Galatians chapter 5. In Galatians 4:6, God makes a connection for us between the Holy Spirit

and Jesus by calling Him the "Spirit of his Son." This same
Spirit brings the fruit of the character of Christ into our lives:
love, joy, peace, patience, kindness, goodness, faithfulness,
gentleness, and self-control (Gal. 5:22-23a). Christ-like character fruit grows over time, all together like one big bunch of
grapes inside the heart of the believer. Apples taste like apples,
grapes taste grapey, and Christ's character fruit in us is Christ-
like. Easton's Bible Dictionary describes character fruit as
"gracious dispositions and habits which the Spirit produces in
those in whom He dwells and works."[10]

Character becomes conduct, as we know, so righteousness
and holy behavior will come, too, in increasing measure.
Philippians 1:11 says we will be filled with the "fruit of righteousness," and Colossians 1:10 issues a call to Christ-followers
to "live a life worthy of the Lord." This sounds impossible if
we really think about it, but remember that Jesus Christ, the
one and only perfect Person, has done it before and can do it
once more inside us. Again, it's a continual interaction
between His Spirit and us, maybe at times feeling more like the
spiritual battle Paul describes raging inside him. "...When I
want to do good, evil is right there with me. For in my inner
being I delight in God's law; but I see another law at work in
the members of my body, waging war against the law of my
mind and making me a prisoner of the law of sin at work
within my members. What a wretched man I am! Who will
rescue me from this body of death? Thanks be to God -
through Jesus Christ our Lord!" (Rom. 7:21-25) Hence, while
sin doesn't completely disappear from our lives, our longing
for or against certain behaviors and temptations will shift
more and more from pain and darkness toward goodness and
light. We surrender control and God lovingly nudges us
toward better things.

Looking ahead a few verses in John 15, we see additionally
that the fruit Christ produces in our lives is "fruit that will last"
(John 15:16). Now, I don't know about the bowl of fruit on

your countertop, but mine doesn't last very long. Our bananas get brown and spotty within a few days, and our strawberries get moldy oftentimes faster than I can cut them up. What Jesus has in mind is fruitfulness that will outlast our lifetimes. He longs to lead others to Himself through you and to produce future generations of Christ-followers that will outlast the present generation on this earth. If you have children of your own, I pray God will allow you to make Him so attractive and real to them that their names will be written in the Lamb's Book of Life alongside yours, as I pray for our own kiddos. I don't think there can be a greater blessing than that for a parent. At the same time, there are spiritual children God wants to place in your life, as well, who will add so much to your life's enjoyment and legacy. Jesus-followers will be used to produce other Jesus-followers. All of this represents fruit that will last.

Only one life, 'twill soon be past. Only what's done for Christ will last. [11]

C.T. Studd

Finally, we'll also make contributions and confessions in life that are fruitful. God has blessed each of us with a given amount of material resources, and He is clear in His Word that His heart is inclined toward the impoverished and marginalized. You and I are to eternally invest our money and material resources, borrowed from the One who gave them to us in the first place, as good and faithful stewards. And if those resources are His, then we should strive to spend them how He would. (See Phil. 4:13-19, Rom. 15:25-28.) Our checkbooks and bank balances will reveal where our treasure is. Scripture says, "For where your treasure is, there your heart will be also." (Matt. 6:21) What contributions are you making with your money and resources? How is God stirring you to meet the earthly needs around you, and what causes do you feel so passionately about that you give freely, regularly, sacrificially, and joyfully of your time and treasures, as though you were giving on behalf of Christ? Your contributions will make a difference to the world around you. Similarly, so will your confession.

What you love, you talk about. Have you ever noticed when you have an amazing meal or experience, you have this insatiable desire inside to tell others about it? It's like your enjoyment of that thing just isn't complete until you've told somebody else about it. As believers, we should feel this same way about praising Jesus. If we really enjoy Jesus, then we won't want to stop gushing about Him until other people know how wonderful He has been in our lives. People who have tasted the goodness of God will tell stories about their experiences to one another. I don't know why talking about matters of faith seems so scary to most of us, but the fruit of our lips is meant to bring a sacrifice of praise (Heb. 13:15, Ps. 34:1). It seems I can hardly talk about my kids or my husband enough because, again, you talk about what you love. Can you relate? If so, let's confess and share Christ, also.

Open your mouth today, believer, and step across that conversational line. I'm telling you, it's very likely God's already put someone in your pathway who needs to hear about Jesus and has tilled the spiritual soil of their heart to be ready. Who knows whether today is that person's last day on this earth? Isn't that possible? It could be instead that they are going through something really heavy in life and need to know God sees them. You are exactly the way whereby God brings them the hope they need. Maybe it's that barista you've been trying to build a relationship with for several years now by going to the same coffee shop day after day. Maybe it's the next-door neighbor for whom you've dropped off dinner or cut the grass. Next time, try to tell them something about the One who has become everything for you. Start somewhere. Trust God. Let His truth and love spill off your tongue, and watch to see what fruit Jesus will bring forth. By the fruit of the branches, the world judges both the Vine and the Gardener.

You, children of God, have been made new. You have a new position, possession, and product in your life as a Christian you didn't have before meeting Jesus. Your identity is not defined by your past mistakes or even your present strivings. It is defined by God and who He says you are. Once you've rested the weight of your whole self in the arms of Jesus Christ, He declares you His own and makes you clean, holy, beloved, and a vessel of His goodness. You'll grow to become more and more like Him everyday. Hear this. Believe it. Bathe in this reality. And while you're busy bathing in the glory of your newness, you may wish to hear a fourth "P" - your *part* in it all.

KEY CONCEPTS

- God is in the business of remaking lives.
- God has a great plan for your life, including your spiritual maturity, a mission in the gospel movement, and a personal ministry of multiplication.
- Your true and lasting identity is found in who God says you are and what He has planned for you.
- If you have placed your faith in Jesus Christ, you are a new creation.
- Your new position as a Jesus-follower is "in Christ." Your new possession is Christ in you. Your life's new product is spiritual fruit that will last.

DISCUSSION QUESTIONS

1. In what ways do you define yourself today? What about others who know you well? What more does God see in you?

2. How has Jesus set you free from the things in life that once had a stronghold on you? Or, how might you need Him to do this now?

3. God sees not only the person you are today, but also the person you are becoming. What excites or scares you most about God's plan for your spiritual maturity, mission in the gospel movement, and personal multiplication through discipleship?

4. Spiritually speaking, is your position today in Adam or in Christ? What next step might you need to take to be sure your position is secure in Jesus Christ?

5. Would you say that your life is characterized by spiritual fruit? Explain.

6. Read the poem *Only One Life* by C. T. Studd in its entirety. Discuss your reactions and reflections.

chapter four

Abiding
daily

Wisdom grows in quiet places. [1]

Austin O'Malley

How do you and I participate in the newness and grace of the gospel? And how can we cultivate this intimate relationship with the very real person of Jesus Christ? You see, all those things we just looked into, your new position, possession, and product, are that which the Lord Himself will accomplish in and through you; but, there is something else new for a Christian, and it's *your part* in the plan of God. The way you'll experience new life in Christ is to faithfully abide with Jesus, to curl up daily in a quiet corner with Him and stoke the fire. You bring the faithfulness, and He'll bring the fruit.

In his book, *Absolute Surrender*, Andrew Murray writes, "You are the branches of the Lord Jesus Christ. If there is in your heart the consciousness that you are not a strong, healthy, fruit-bearing branch, not closely linked with Jesus, not living in Him as you should be - then listen to Him say: 'I am the Vine, I will receive you, I will draw you to myself, I will bless you, I will strengthen you, I will fill you with my Spirit. I, the Vine, have taken you to be my branches, I have given myself utterly to you; children, give yourselves utterly to me. I have surrendered myself as God absolutely to you; I became man and died for you that I might be entirely yours. Come and surrender yourselves entirely to be mine.'"[2]

In the vine-and-branches teaching of Jesus in John 15, there is only one command found in that passage for us to receive and obey. Nine times in those eleven verses, Jesus expressed the word "abide" or remain, *menō* in the original Greek. Since it's repeated so many times, this concept is obviously something to which we need to pay attention. Let's do a quick dictionary crosscheck and uncover a baseline definition of abiding.

abide
verb \ ə-'bīd \
to wait for; to accept without objection; to remain
    stable or fixed in a state; to continue in a place[3]
to remain; sojourn; tarry; not to depart; to continue to
    be present; to be held or kept continually; to live;
    to remain as one; to wait for[4]

CULTIVATING AFFECTION
What a rich word! To abide in Christ is to remain in connection with Him and to be fully present in order to enjoy God's company, wisdom, and grace. Abiding, then, means being held by Jesus, both in the present and for all eternity. It's within the context of a relationship that Jesus can affirm our

forgiveness and worth, and where He makes our hearts full with love.

A friend and fellow disciple once told me she was sitting in her living room one evening, scrolling away on her phone, when one of her children asked her a question. She glanced up and provided an answer to the question, all the while still swiping around on the little piece of glass in front of her. Her little babe asked another question, and she repeated as before. Finally, her little one took her chubby, little hands, placed them on her momma's cheeks, and guided her eyes upward to meet her own. Real love demands attention. It needs it. It deserves it. While God won't force us to be with Him, He deserves nothing less. And He wants nothing more.

Many times we try to create a relationship with Jesus by taking part in everything we see other Christians doing; and for those of us in the modern-day evangelical culture, that means serving coffee on Sundays, making casseroles, being at church every time the doors are open, attending one Bible study after another, and saying "yes" to everything else we are asked to do. No question, those things are all good things. Let me just say while I prefer veggies to most casseroles, I really do love coffee and Bible study, as you've probably picked up on. As a matter of fact, if you put them together, time spent in scripture *with* coffee and friends is one of my very favorite things in all the world to do. Still, is this do-it-all approach how we cultivate intimacy in our other relationships? Do we sign up for committees and burn our candles from end to end in order to grow in affection with our spouse, close friends, or family? Of course not. Remember, God is not after our attempts to make fruit in the first place; that's His miracle to perform. On the contrary, He's after our willingness to stay close to Him, to rest in Him, and to trust Him. Therefore, as we approach our relationship with Christ, as with our other friendships, there must be ongoing, two-way communication and personal time spent together for the relationship to bud with affection.

This is why scripture calls us, the Church, the Bride of Christ and likens our spiritual relationship with Him to that of a bride and groom. Before we move on, let's just be clear: no marriage is perfect. Not one. Not the one you have, not the ones you see, and not the one you might be dreaming of if you are single. Even that married couple that always seems to have it all together - you know, the ones with matching outfits and googoo eyes all the time. Even them; not perfect. We are sinful, selfish people, so putting two of any of us together in one home, sharing life, is hard as often as it is wonderful. There are happy days in marriage and times that are picture frame worthy, and then there are other days that you just want to forget. Jon and I have experienced all of these in our sixteen years of marriage, including times when we've wondered if it's going to work at all and other days when our hearts have leapt off the ground.

Your romance with Christ will follow suit. Jesus is steady, loving, and selfless all the time. He is forgiving and gentle and has constant surprises up His sleeve to thrill and delight your heart. You, however, still bring self-centered tendencies and a wandering heart into the equation, so there will be ups and downs, highs and lows. In your walk with God, you will have days that feel spiritually dry and lonely, likely because you've wandered away or lack awareness about how God is working through your circumstances, and you'll have other days when you can't wait to tell others about how God has thrilled you to the core. For a married couple, marriage is a commitment remade again and again with each new day, and your spiritual relationship with Jesus must also be patiently stoked through daily abiding.

YOUR BEST YES

There is good work to be done in the name of Jesus (Eph. 2:8-10), special tasks you are uniquely created to do that bring glory and honor to the name of God. A few reminders, though:

- You cannot and should not do this work on your own.
- You need God's power and wisdom.
- Every job is not meant for you to fill.

A friend recently reminded me that sometimes we all need to say "no" to some things in order to offer our best "yes" to the right things. So, as you pull up your chair to the table with Jesus, you must deliberately set aside everything you think you bring to that table, your own perceived strengths, merits, and aspirations, in order to draw everything from the Lord. God alone is to be your source of power and strength.

I envision a sewing machine as a helpful illustration for this abiding connection. When you look at a working sewing machine (never mind the dust collecting on mine), the needle is where your eyes are drawn. All the action and excitement is naturally found at the needle's edge. Up-and-down, side-to-side, the needle has all the fun. Allow your eyes, though, to wander just a foot or two away and observe the power plug. It appears rather boring, I'm sure we'd all agree, but frankly it's where all the power comes from to create the movement that's so captivating. There is a constant connection with Christ in your life that must be found for God's power to flow in and through you. This is abiding. Resist the swirl and glitter of the world around you, which clamors after your time and atten-tion every time you might otherwise draw near to God. Come to Him, instead, in order to be fully equipped, rested, and ready for all the marvelous things you were made to do.

Success isn't what you've done compared to others. Success is what you've done compared to what you were made to do.[5]

Lecrae Moore

RESPONSIBLE TO ABIDE

For many of us, just like with the topic of marriage, the "grass is greener" syndrome of comparison returns to invade our minds when we consider our own personal ministry. Again, I know there are certain believers who always appear to you and me as if they have it all together. They're wise and well-liked, their prayers sound like poetry, and their ministry seems more sparkly than ours. But if there is no personal abiding when the curtain is drawn back, in their lives or in ours, then it's all a shiny facade masking religious behavior and continual striving for acceptance and worth. We need grace. We *all* need grace. We need to sit in the lap of our loving Father and to feel His embrace. Every. Single. Day. And the overflow of this time with our First Love is what fuels and gives shape to our ministry inside and outside of our homes.

Let me say it another way. Your life's work is the overflow of God's work in you. So you can stop playing the comparison game. You're not here to make yourself look good. And you're not here to out-serve others. You're here to fall in love with God daily and let His love spill over onto a needy world in every corner of society, and it will take all of us working together to accomplish this. Knowing this should bring sweet relief, a deep breath that allows the weight of exhaustion and envy to roll off your shoulders. You are responsible to abide. God is responsible for the rest. The same goes for me. All the glory is due Him.

ADVENTURES UNTOLD

One of my most valued earthly treasures is my backpack, covered with world flags and patches from past adventures. As with all memories, some of these have been monumental and others, honestly, pretty wretched. Life and this backpack have led me up rugged South American peaks, along breathtaking historical ruins, and into world-renowned art museums. Other patches recall nightmares of trailborn illness, treacherous white-water escapes, and close-calls with wild lions and elephants on safari. Even with all these adventures in tow, still today my mind swirls with wonder imagining what untold adventures lie ahead.

The Christian life, truly lived, is an exciting adventure, at minimum. With such a vast world to explore, how could any of us ever resign ourselves to boredom? I heard a pastor recently say in a Sunday sermon that it would be impossible for a Christian to be bored if he or she is really walking with Jesus. So true! The Lion of Judah is anything but tame. How often, though, do we really drop our fishing nets and leave everything known, comfortable, and safe behind in order to follow Jesus *wherever* He will lead?

Adventures lie around every corner. What will you say to that next person along your path today who is willing to engage with you in a conversation about God? Where might God lead you in this great big world to make His gospel known and to serve others with extravagant love? It could be next door, at work, in the market, over the tracks, or across the ocean that the Lord chooses to use you. Count them all adventures. I urge you to put your best "yes" on the table in full surrender, and to let God put it on the map. Walking with God into the unknown is bound to be an adventure like no other. Listen, though, you have no truth to speak nor a trail map to follow if you are not reading God's Word and abiding daily with Jesus. I repeat, this is where the power is found. Just like that sewing machine plug, steady in its socket, your relationship with the Lord must be firmly rooted and kindled daily. First John 2:28 (ESV) teaches, "And now little children, abide in Christ, that when he shall appear, we may have confidence and not be ashamed before him at his coming." Very soon we will all see Jesus face to face. On that day, may each of us stand on *familiar*, holy ground.

YOUR DAILY QUIET TIME WITH GOD

It will sound as if I'm kidding, but one of the toughest classes I took as an undergrad was a SCUBA class. Coach Billy, a man teeming with life and gusto, taught me to become one with my diving equipment. During one of the toughest exercises of the class, we student divers were put through a rigorous test known as "Do or Die." Sounds fun, right? After jumping into the deep end of a pool with full gear on and sinking down to the depths, teaching assistants spun us around in circles until up and down made no sense anymore. They pulled off our face masks, snatched the tanks from our backs, and twisted and tugged our gear until we proved we could calmly survive any unexpected underwater scenario. During a similar test, we traveled down and back underwater, taking just one breath of air midway across the pool for what seemed like forever. I remember my lungs felt like they might implode, and yet a mind-over-matter philosophy somehow enabled me to gently kick and glide until that next breath filled the balloon inside my chest. The training was beyond difficult, and at the moment I thought I might not make it, however it helped me develop the skills I needed to meet any danger that real open-water dives might present.

In preparing to explore the sea, a good diver wouldn't dream of dropping off the side of a boat without first checking their gear for a solid connection between their air source and mouth. Similarly, as a Christian you shouldn't jump into the deep of your day without first making a solid connection with the Lord through your daily quiet time. After all, He is Himself the Author of the day and the one who gives you your very life's breath. This alone time with God will equip you for all the twists, turns, and opportunities that lie ahead. God wrote the story of this day in His book before time began, and He awaits your pause to share just what you need to hear before charging onward. There is no other way for you to truly be prepared, apart from God Himself doing the preparing. What, then, should this alone time look like? And, how important is it to your walk with Jesus?

YOUR GREATEST PRIORITY

Previously, we touched upon an important concept: you make time for the things that are most important to you. Time alone with Jesus is vital to your life as a Christian and, there-fore, it must be a priority. I've personally struggled with making it my top priority on many occasions. On days when I jumped right into the waters on my own, I found that life quickly unraveled for me. I was not equipped to handle the day's challenges in my own strength. Sometimes my words quickly turned unkind, my patience became short, and my emotions spiraled out of control. The waves rolled in, whether parenting frustrations, the stress of hurrying, or the weight of heavy burdens, and I was undone before the morning was through. I wonder if you've ever felt this way. On the other hand, there have been days when I succeeded shaking off my pillow in order to run to Christ first. On mornings like those, when Jesus gave me exactly the truth I needed for the day ahead, the fruit of the Spirit of Christ dwelled in my heart. As a result, my knee-jerk reactions to the waves subsided, and God filled me with enough patience, love, and joy to go around. Experience proved that being with God needs to be my foremost priority everyday, regardless of the way my to-do lists and snooze button threaten to capsize my wakeup routine.

PERIOD & PLACE

After considering time with God as your highest priority, what about the time period and place where your alone time with the Lord should be spent? Jesus rose early in the morning, before the sun was up, and started his day by going off to a solitary place to pray (Mark 1:35). Later, just before demonstrating His model prayer known to many of us as "The Lord's Prayer" (Matt. 6:9-13), Jesus told His disciples to go into a room, close the door, and pray to the Father in private (Matt. 6:6). These truths suggest our ideal quiet time with God will be in the morning and we should go somewhere we can feel undistracted and close to God.

Remember, too, the Israelites gathered manna in the desert as their "daily bread," which God required to be gathered fresh each morning in order to keep from spoiling. As the true Manna to come, Jesus said that man doesn't live by bread alone but by every word that comes from the mouth of God (Matt. 4:4), so His Word is *our* daily bread. It's our spiritual nourishment, and it should be gathered fresh every day. Yesterday's manna is not meant for today.

Now, if you lump yourself into the category of "night owl," while I can't say my eyelids and circadian rhythm agree with yours, I would offer that you should make the spiritual rhythms of your day work best for you, whatever that looks like on the clock. Jesus fought His greatest battle on His knees in the Garden of Gethsemane during the late hours of the night, so clearly there is biblical precedent for nighttime prayer too.

However you work it, like the diver and the air hose, just be sure you feel prepared for the day ahead by the One who has written it into place (see Ps. 139:16).

In the morning, O Lord, you hear my voice; in the morning I lay my requests before you and wait in expectation.

Psalm 5:3

Satisfy us in the morning with your unfailing love, that we may sing for joy and be glad all our days.

Psalm 90:14

A NOTE ON PARENTING

Whether you have kids, hope to have kids one day, or know someone with kids, let's chat about the life of a disciple with littles for a moment. Whatever your stage of life, either you or someone you know will need encouragement when it comes to building rhythms of devotion with small children. Let's imagine you've been up all night with a newborn, a sick kiddo, or one who has wet the bed yet again. How do you pop out of bed to run to Jesus when you can hardly open your eyelids? First, grace. Immerse yourself in God's grace, breathing it in as you pause in your exhaustion, knowing He is with you always and that your performance, even in your daily quiet time, does not in any way determine your value in God's eyes or the unfathomable love He feels toward you. God's mighty purposes prevail over your life, even when you struggle to steal a few moments away to read, reflect, study, or pray. In these seasons, consider setting your Bible or a devotional near your late night post, write scripture on notecards to set in snuggly spaces, or sing hymns and spiritual songs that draw you and your little love close to the King.

Your strategies will inevitably need to be adjusted over

time. As your little ones grow and begin to tiptoe down the hallway even earlier, and you just can't seem to wake up early enough anymore, then welcome them in and read aloud instead. Let their little eyes and ears join you at the foot of the throne of grace. At nap time, if you're lucky enough that your kids still take one, try offering the "first fruits" of this part of your day to the Lord. Oftentimes you'll find God will honor this sacrifice by somehow making those naps last a little bit longer, or the endless laundry piles somehow shrink and get done anyhow.

Your irregular daily routine might not be today what you hope it will one day become, but choosing God in the moments available to you will fill your heart with hope, your mind with needed truth, and your mouth with His gracious kindness. Press on with Jesus. Inhale scripture with all the energy and brain power you can muster. Let others who have made it through the fog of early parenting encourage *you* in this time. Open your life and home to younger disciples, as well, who can simultaneously serve you and learn from you. While it feels so tirelessly long, this time of your life will indeed be fleeting, and you'll one day remember it with fondness, and perhaps a little laughter, too.

One final thought on time. Many of us wonder how long is long enough for our daily quiet time with God. The answer is, ideally, enough time to forget about time. Having said that, though, start with just five to ten minutes. Once five minutes isn't enough anymore, simply give yourself more time. This is the magic of enjoying time alone with God; the more you have, the more you'll want. Unlike other things in life, this is one area where your indulgence will be life-giving.

MEET MORGAN

Morgan, a fellow disciple-maker and dear friend of mine, shared with me that early on in her discipleship journey with me she was reflecting on how long to spend during her personal quiet time in the mornings. The next morning, Morgan prayed and jumped into reading her Bible, right where she left off the day before. She decided to keep reading that day until God made it clear it was time to stop and move on with her day. After studying her Bible awhile, she landed on John 14:31, "Come now; let us leave." She knew, then and there, God was saying it was time to move into the day together. Ha! How about that? God met with her and answered her question right there in His own Word. The Word of God is alive and active (Heb. 4:12), always relevant for whatever you're facing. So, like Morgan, next time you're tossing off your pillow and snuggling up with Jesus in the morning, set a goal of allowing yourself enough time to forget about time. Start with a few minutes, and add more when you are ready.

INGREDIENTS

Like the baker or chef handcrafting a small batch master-piece, you'll want to gather the right ingredients for a satis-fying quiet time experience. What ingredients, or resources, will you need for your daily quiet time with God? Begin with a Bible, a journal, and a pen or pencil as the very essentials. Adding to that list, you might also consider a daily devotional or reading plan, prayer list, and a globe, map or international prayer guide such as *Operation World*. Another go-to resource might be the *Blue Letter Bible* app, which offers definitions, pronunciations, and insights about the text in which each passage of scripture was originally spoken or written, such as Hebrew or Greek. *BLB* is the perfect aid to help you discover what God really means in a passage you're reading, rather than what you would otherwise conveniently read into the text or interpret on your own. Finally, consider using the *Faithlife Study Bible* app, which provides rich historical and cultural context through commentaries, infographics, and videos that can help you feel like you're set right inside the scene of biblical times. Ask yourself how the original readers or hearers would have interpreted a passage of scripture. It's very likely digging into their cultural context can bring a whole new meaning to what you're reading you might not have ever considered. Start here. Using good ingredients like these as you study the Word of God will help you hear from God with greater clarity and better understand His heart. One word of caution for you and your small batch: don't let any supporting resources themselves (including this book) replace your Bible. Your Bible is your love letter from the Lord and the only truly essential ingredient. Read it daily.

Have you ever received a love letter? Knowing how I adore words of affirmation, at one point early in our marriage, Jon wrote a daily love note to me in a little black book three months straight, until every page was filled, which he presented to me on our anniversary. That'll fill a girl's love tank for a while! Though I'm not certain about her preferences, just before they married, Samuel Clemens (aka Mark Twain) wrote a love letter to his bride-to-be, Olivia Langdon, that would melt the butter off a piece of toast. "Out of the depths of my happy heart wells a great tide of love and prayer for this priceless treasure that is confined to my life-long keeping. You cannot see its intangible waves as they flow towards you, darling, but in these lines you will hear, as it were, the distant beating of the surf."[6] Words like these would be read again and again and held close to the chest for a life-time. If you'll allow the Holy Spirit of God to bring His Word to life for you personally each day, you'll want to do the very same with your Bible. It is indeed God's love letter, the story of His passionate pursuit of your heart, every page dripping with affection. Hold it close always.

While certainly not a requirement, you may find it a nice touch to light your favorite candle during your morning quiet time and allow the "fragrance of Christ" (2 Cor. 2:15) to linger with you throughout the day. It's also possible to tuck away your quiet time materials in a basket near where you meet with Jesus, and to tie a camouflage bandana around the handle of your basket to remind you to fight for this time. Paul David Tripp reminds us that, "In our everyday lives, the Kingdom of God and the kingdom of self are always at war with one another."[7] Fight the good fight, beloved.

PRACTICE

Now, regarding the practice of having a daily quiet time, what do you actually *do*? Follow these three simple steps:

1. Talk with God.
2. Read His Word.
3. Think about it throughout your day.

That's it! God promises to be present with you, His beloved child, when you seek Him. Therefore, however your day unfolds, once you set your Bible back in your basket, you can rest assured knowing God is near.

Your daily quiet time is the best time to align your heart with God's heart. Ask God to help you have on your heart what is on His. Seek God's Spirit to illuminate scripture and unfold its truth for you (Ps. 119:18, 130). Perhaps think about beholding God in some new way, believing in Him and falling more in love with Him. Like the father in Mark 9:24 (ESV) said to Jesus, "I believe; help my unbelief!" Believe. Be held. Rest your burdens and worries for the day in the arms of your Savior. Like Mary, treasure God's Word and turn it around in your mind (Luke 2:19). Be willing to obey whatever the Lord shows you during your time together. Then, step into your day with Jesus.

Then King David went in and sat before the Lord…

2 Sam. 7:18

Be still, and know that I am God…

Ps. 46:10 (ESV)

Open my eyes that I may see wonderful things in your law.

Ps. 119:18

The unfolding of your words gives light; it gives understanding to the simple.

Ps. 119:130

There are several additional prayer and Bible study techniques that may help you continue to grow your quiet time practice. We'll look at some of these in depth in the next section of the book.

PURPOSE

Let's back up a moment to also consider the "why" of your daily alone time with Jesus. What's the purpose of this time? James 1:5 instructs, "If any of you lacks wisdom, you should ask God, who gives generously to all without finding fault, and it will be given to you." As a disciple, it's in your daily quiet time where God's wisdom is found.

Moses once stood on what the Bible describes as "holy ground" and heard the voice of God calling from within a burning bush (Exod. 3). As he wandered with his father-in-law's sheep to the far side of the desert, Moses approached Mount Sinai. A strange sight caught his eye, a bush on fire but not burning up. Obviously curious about this, he walked over to see it. Moses turned aside from what he was doing. Then, having captured his attention, God spoke to Moses. God told him many things about Himself, about how He was concerned for His people, and about His special purposes for Moses. What a beautiful picture of the purpose of your daily quiet time with God! Although you're not likely to hear God's voice coming from inside your garden hedges, you are, like Moses, to turn aside and allow God to reveal Himself to you.

Interestingly, if you keep reading this story, you'll find Moses was afraid and felt unqualified for the job ahead. Moses talked to God about his worries, and God helped him come up with a specific plan for how he would accomplish all he was called to do. God said, "Now go; I will help you to speak and will teach you what to say" (Exod. 4:10-12). Moses pleaded with God to send someone else. There were many ups and downs that followed because of Moses' fear and lack of confidence to speak in public. Graciously, God granted Moses a ministry partner to help him, his brother Aaron (vv. 13-17), and over time Moses became a great spokesman of God before the nation of Israel, God's people. In one of the mightiest moments of Moses' ministry, God entrusted Moses with the Ten Commandments, etched on new stone tablets after the first ones were destroyed. Then God passed by Moses and allowed him to catch a glimpse of His glory. As a sign of His presence and pleasure, God caused Moses' face to reflect His glory as he made his way back down the mountain toward the people (Exod. 33-34). His face was literally shiny and bright, and the people were both amazed and afraid when they saw him. Moses comforted the people and called them to come near, sharing with them what God had told him. Finally, Moses put a veil over his face until the next time he went to speak with the Lord. Second Corinthians 3:13 explains that Moses was afraid for the people to notice how God's glory was fading between visits and that they would "see the end of what was passing away."

You, too, reflect the Lord's glory as you enjoy His presence. Others will know when you've been with Jesus, who has Himself become for us wisdom from God (1 Cor. 1:30), and you'll need to go back to Him regularly just like Moses did. Over time, by continuing to meet with Jesus during your daily quiet time, you'll grow in His likeness, all shiny and bright.

And we, who with unveiled faces all reflect the Lord's glory, are being transformed into his likeness with ever-increasing glory, which comes from the Lord, who is the Spirit.

2 Cor. 3:18

Quite the opposite of Moses was the prophet Elijah. In his rampant confidence and readiness to run out and speak to others on behalf of God, Elijah was led by the Lord to a remote place called the Kerith Ravine (Kerith meaning "to cut off"). He was cut off for a time from everything he had and all the people and places he once knew (1 Kings 17-18). Elijah drew water from a brook nearby and was fed by ravens at God's direction, a scavenger species of bird normally considered unclean by Jewish people like him. (Note of interest: a group of ravens is called an "unkindness," and yet God's kindness to Elijah was delivered through such a bird!) Some time later, the brook dried up, and God led Elijah to a new place, where he was used by God to nourish a despairing mother and her son just before they would have starved. Talk about experiencing God at work! After three years tucked away and depending on the Lord, Elijah was finally ready to again present himself to King Ahab and speak on God's behalf. Elijah provides this vital lesson for us: as you seek to do God's work and share His glory with the world, you'll need to hide yourself in God's presence before you present yourself to others on His behalf (see 1 Kings 17:3, 18:1). Wherever you find yourself spiritually today, questioning whether God can use you at all or hastily grabbing life by the horns, your quiet time with the Lord is essential.

At one point in my life with two tiny little ones at home, I made it my goal to seek the face of God before I saw the face of another person. I wanted so badly to sit with the Lord in order to feel more prepared to be a gracious and loving momma with the Word of God on my heart. Since it was nearly impossible to sneak downstairs without waking our kids, I soon found myself huddling with God in our actual closet. One morning, I felt especially lonely. I remember longing to feel loved and recognized, but instead I felt isolated and unimportant. Pushing aside dirty laundry piles to find just enough space, I crouched down on my knees in my closet and discovered God was right there with me. In this tiny, crowded spot, the Lord met with me, dirty laundry and all. As I prayed, the poem by Robert Browning, which was read in our wedding ceremony, echoed in my heart. "Grow old along with me! The best is yet to be, the last of life, for which the first was made."[8] I'd always hoped Jon would feel this way about me at every turn along our marriage journey, but the emotional needs I felt in this season of life were so great they could only have been met by a perfect and inexhaustible love. No human being can ever fully meet our emotional or physical needs, and Heaven knows I still fall short of this for my beloved all the time. So on this day, right when I needed to hear it, God impressed upon me that *He* felt this way about me. I could sense His arms almost tangibly wrapped around me. He loved me big time, had great plans in store for the rest of my life, and looked forward to walking those special purposes out by my side. Maybe you need to hear this, too. There is One who can meet every deep desire of your heart, and the marvelous thing is He also *wants* to! I'm not sure what your deepest needs are today, but I do know our God is very real, and He will meet you right where you are if you will pause, turn aside, and seek Him.

You will seek me and find me when you seek me with all your heart.

Jeremiah 29:13

PROTECTION

Protect this time in your day. Guard it from the enemy who fully knows its importance; there will be distractions and spiritual attacks that tug at your desire to meet with God. God awaits you, wants to be with you, and has so much to show you. Run to him! Take God up on his invitation to you. You will never regret one minute spent with Jesus.

KEY CONCEPTS

- Your part to play in experiencing new life in Christ is to faithfully abide with Jesus. If you do, He will cause spiritual fruit to grow.
- An intimate relationship with Jesus is cultivated through regular communication and time spent together.
- Spending time with God should be your first and greatest priority.
- Your daily quiet time is the chance to turn aside and allow God to reveal Himself to you.
- Set aside enough time during your daily quiet time to forget about time.
- When reading your Bible, the cultural context and original language of a passage of scripture provide

greater understanding about the meaning of the text.

DISCUSSION QUESTIONS

1. Have you recently been more focused on your own fruitfulness or faithfulness? How might it lighten your burden to remember that your part in God's work in and through your life is to abide daily with Him?
2. Do you struggle with comparing yourself to others? Explain. What is one thing God's Word says about you that you can cling to for encouragement when you feel you don't measure up?
3. What has been your greatest adventure so far in life? Are you being nudged by God toward any new adventures now?
4. Do you need to make time with God and reading His Word a greater priority? Explain why or why not.
5. What barriers or interruptions make it difficult for you to focus on God?
6. Share an example of a time when God revealed something to you through His Word that was exactly what you needed to hear that day.

chapter five

Loving God:
bible study & prayer

"...Of all the commandments, which is the most important?" "The most important one," answered Jesus, "is this: Hear, O Israel: The Lord our God, the Lord is one. Love the Lord your God with all your heart and with all your soul and with all your mind and with all your strength. The second is this: Love your neighbor as yourself..."

Mark 12:28-31

American football is a sport that has always excited a crowd. Players and fans alike have enjoyed the thrill of victory and felt the agony of defeat. Paul William "Bear" Bryant was an American college football player and coach, best known as the head coach of the University of Alabama football team. During his 25-year tenure at Alabama, he accrued six national titles and 15 conference championships, and he retired in 1982 with the most wins as head coach in collegiate football history - 323.[1] His legacy has lived on through the years. As a matter of fact, if you've ever experienced a 'Bama football game in person or on television, you undoubtedly noticed the sea of houndstooth print throughout the grandstands — another mark of the coach's enduring legacy. How did he create an environment for so much victory? While explaining his coaching philosophy and the lessons learned through all his years of coaching, Bryant simply stated, "Everyone works hard on the big things. Don't forget the little things, the fundamentals that win games."[2]

Discipleship is like this: it's often the little things that count the most. Jesus wants to remind us of this basic truth. He puts us on the same team. Then, you and I build one another up in the fundamentals of our faith; loving God and loving others. Jesus said these two things are to be seen together as the greatest commandment for God's people, and therefore they'll serve as the foundations of a discipleship journey for Jesus' followers. We'll focus in our small batches on living these out in the ways Jesus and His first followers did in the Bible - *loving God* through studying the Bible and praying, and *loving others* by talking about God, cultivating authentic relationships with other believers, and serving people with compassion.

MEET KAYLA

Kayla served on the campus ministry team at the university she attended. Early in her college career, she made it her personal mission to share the good news of Jesus with other students and to disciple any who came to faith. At one point, another student made a decision to follow Jesus, so Kayla and a friend immediately took her under their wings and walked with her as she got to know Jesus. Early in their journey together, she told them, "I'm not sure if I'm really a Christian." They asked why she felt that way, and she responded, "I'm just not sure I'm doing all the things I'm supposed to be doing right." Many others have probably wondered this same thing, but wouldn't it be great if every new believer had someone *show* them how to personally and practically walk out their faith in a hands-on, up-close-and-personal way like Kayla did?

We who follow Jesus are to do exactly what these campus missionaries did, pointing others to God by caring for them as people, sharing our own stories of faith with them, and opening the Word of God together so they can hear His voice for themselves. We need to create safe spaces where others can ask their biggest, hairiest questions without judgment and find honest answers in God's Word they can take to the bank. Then, when they're ready, we can come alongside those who choose to follow Jesus and help them stand firmly in the foundations of the Christian faith. Ultimately, once they're standing firmly on their own, we are to cheer them along in whatever direction God leads them into the future and equip them to do the same thing for others as they're going.

We'll use a cross as a helpful illustration for the four foundations, or key components, of the Christian life. After all, everything that matters for all eternity in the life of a Christian begins at the foot of the cross of Calvary. Imagine a cross shaped like a lowercase letter "t". In the center of the cross is the name of "Jesus" because the Person of Jesus is to be at the very center of your life. A vertical beam stretches up and down, representing your relationship with God, and a horizontal beam extends from side-to-side, symbolizing your relationship with others. The vertical beam, the personal connection between you and God, is the anchor to your entire journey.

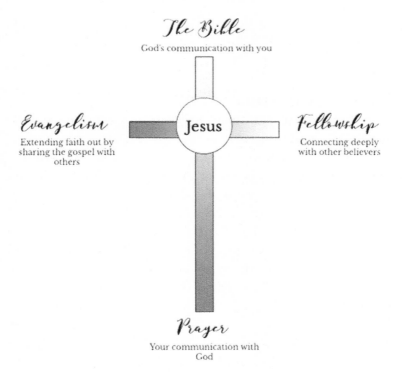

The Bible
God's communication with you

Evangelism
Extending faith out by
sharing the gospel with
others

Jesus

Fellowship
Connecting deeply
with other believers

Prayer
Your communication with
God

In order for a cross to remain upright, it has to be firmly rooted in the ground. The horizontal beam can't hang in midair without the vertical beam holding strong and steady, right? So it is with your spiritual life. Your personal relationship with God supports the weight of your life as a believer, and you develop this relationship through ongoing communication between the two of you. Coming down from the top of the cross is the Word of God, your spiritual intake. God speaks to you, His child, through the Bible. Prayer, then, reaches from the ground up. God speaks to you, and you respond back to Him. It's a conversation. Conversations are how relationships are born, and continual conversation is how they grow into the most intimate friendships; into love. This connection is the very foundation of your faith as a believer.

You desperately need a loving relationship with God, and He has already reached out to you to initiate the conversation.

LOVING GOD: BIBLE STUDY

When God speaks, things happen. In the beginning, God spoke the world into creation. He opened His mouth and... bang! Life. His Word is mighty and powerful. His Word is important. While it's true that the wonders of nature illuminate God's truths in spectacular ways every day, the Bible is in fact the primary way God speaks today. Hebrews 4:12 proclaims that, "The Word of God is alive and active." It's the source of all truth, which saves and sanctifies (see 1 Pet. 1:23 and Rom. 10:17). It's the spiritual milk for babes in Christ to grow on (1 Pet. 2:2), a juicy t-bone steak as you begin to mature. God's Word guides you as you learn to walk out your faith and as you grow in understanding (Ps. 119:105, 130). It cleanses you and frees you from those things that might harm you (John 15:3, Eph. 5:26, Heb. 4:12). On the journey of life, it's a must-have. You need regular contact with scripture.

Remember, the "seed" is the Word of God (Luke 8:11) and the "field" is the world (Matt. 13:38). As a Christ follower, do what Jesus did with scripture; know it in your mind, stow it deep within your heart, show it by walking it out in obedience every day, and sow it by flinging seed indiscriminately, sharing His truth with others.

> *Preach the word; be prepared in season and out of season;*
> *correct, rebuke and encourage — with great patience and*
> *careful instruction.*

> 2 Timothy 4:2

Those who go out weeping, carrying seed to sow, will return with songs of joy, carrying sheaves with them.

Psalm 126:6

As you read the Bible, strive to be a student of the text, digging in with both hands to discover the truest and deepest meaning behind each passage. Use the tools mentioned earlier when we discussed having a daily quiet time, and share those tools with anyone you disciple. Now, let's pretend we're sitting across a table from one another or side-by-side on a sofa and get really practical about this. It's time to build upon what we learned previously. I'll walk you through studying your own Bible one step at a time.

- Pray.

First, begin in prayer. Ask God to light up His Word for you and show you something you don't already know. Check out at Psalm 119:18, 130 and Jeremiah 33:3 for inspiration on how to pray something like this.

- Read God's Word.

Next, open your Bible and read a passage of scripture. You can work your way bit-by-bit through an entire book, such as the gospel of Mark, or read one Psalm each day, for example. Read it, then open your *FaithLife Study Bible* app and review contextual information for the passage you just read. Return to the verses and take notes in your Bible about what you learned. Mark it up. Make it *yours* so that one day when you re-read the same scripture, you'll be able to pull treasures out of your spiritual storehouse and remember what God once revealed to you. To take it one step further, if a word stands out to you in the text, look it up in the concordance section of your *Blue Letter Bible* app and see what additional insight God provides. Digging in like this is where your conversation with the Lord becomes even more profitable. Don't shortchange yourself.

- Reflect on what you read.

Take time to think about what you've just learned. Turn it around in your mind. Process it. Remember it. Write your thoughts down in a journal if you'd like. Whatever helps you most, be sure to connect your reading back to your life. How might God's Word strengthen you emotionally today? Where do you need to be challenged by God? What should you share with someone else as a source of encouragement?

- Pray again.

Finish your time in prayer. Thank God for illuminating scripture and inviting you in. Ask Him to help you walk out His commands with obedience as you leave this moment and take on the day. Amen!

MEET RACHEL

Rachel enjoyed a quiet time in just this same way. God showed her something in the morning uniquely meant to equip her for the day ahead. She explored a Bible verse she'd committed to memorize over the course of the month, "The Lord will fight for you; you need only to be still" (Exod. 14:14). Rachel pulled out her study tools to better understand the deeper meaning of *fight for you*, as well as what it meant to *be still*. She had a sneaking suspicion God didn't mean she should literally sit on the couch all day, which was good because her day was already looking pretty full. Her suspicion was correct. She learned by studying this verse that God would fight her

Loving God: Bible Study and Prayer   123

battles, defend her, and He would prevail. She also learned
that the call to *be still* meant to be quiet and peaceful, to hold
her tongue when it felt like war was waging around her,
and to cease fighting. Big ideas!

Rachel took those nuggets with her as she went on with
her day, and as you might have guessed, they really came in
handy. As it turns out, Rachel had a tear-stained conversation
late in the day with a colleague who believed she had been
secretly gossiping about her. On the contrary, she'd actually
been working hard to build relational bridges at work by
meeting with various coworkers who seemed at odds with one
another and trying to serve as a mediator. Unfortunately for
Rachel, her good intentions at peacemaking were misinter-
preted. Maybe you've experienced a similar scenario, where
your best intentions just didn't play out the way you expected?

Looking back, it's uncanny what the Lord had shown her
during her quiet time that same morning. God prepared
Rachel's heart for this situation by telling her in advance to
bite her tongue, to allow Him to fight her battles, and to root
herself deeply in the Lord. He said He would fight for her if
she would only be still. Remembering that promise helped
Rachel respond better in this situation than she would have
otherwise, and rather than reacting with raw emotions and a
defensive attitude, she sat down and listened. She made a
point to understand the other person's emotional experience.
When it was her turn, she shared her own perspective and
apologized for the way this whole situation had made her
coworker feel. They were able to move forward. Truth be told,
it wasn't about Rachel anyhow. It wasn't about defending
herself or her reputation. In the grand scheme of things, she
was there to represent God and to love others well. What a
great reminder that time alone in God's Word can help
prepare any of us for the things we simply can't see coming.

If you're already enjoying a strong rhythm with your quiet
time practice, then I encourage you to wade into the

spiritual waters one step deeper. In the United States, the grading system in schools is based upon a student's G.P.A., or grade point average. And of course in academics, it's often true that good study habits lead to a good G.P.A. The same can be said for you as a student of scripture. When you're studying your Bible, you might think about looking for the G.P.A. in your daily reading.

- First, where do you see **God (G)**, and what is He revealing to you about Himself?
- Second, where do you see mankind or **people (P)**, and what does the passage you're reading reveal about you and me?
- Third, what is an **application (A)** you can make to your everyday life based on what you've read? In other words, what should your response be to what God's Word is showing you today? Is there a promise to cling to? Is there a lesson to learn or a mistake to avoid? Has God uncovered an area of sin in your life that you need help with? Maybe He's asking you to reach out to lovingly serve others in a new way. Whatever the case, God has a message uniquely meant for you today, and you'll miss out if you pass it by.

As I write this, it's been awhile since my last meal, and I'm feeling hungry. Compared to many people around the world who don't, I'm lucky to have food to eat today. I've noticed that when I make good, healthy choices with the foods I eat, I feel better physically and have more energy to enjoy my daily activities. Of course, the opposite is also true that when I grab a junky snack, like potato chips, I feel awful and am filled with regret. God's Word is like your spiritual food (Job 23:12, Jer. 15:16). It strengthens you and gives you the boost you need to live this life well. What are you filling your inner self up with?

Don't try to quench the hunger of your heart with the garbage of this world; instead, feast on the Word of God and be satisfied. It's right there waiting for you, and it covers every practical little detail of life you'll encounter today.

DIAMONDS

God's Word teaches us as Jesus-followers to live our lives well and honor God with what we say and do. None of us does this perfectly, though. Therefore, other times God's Word leads us back onto the straight and narrow after we've gone astray. I remember a time like this when God's Word helped me make a major course correction after I failed to tell the truth.

Years ago, Jon gave me a beautiful diamond pendant as an anniversary gift. It was a big sacrifice for us financially at the time, and I was honored to wear it. I forgot to call our insurance agent to have it added to our insurance policy right away. The very next day, I ventured out at the "golden hour" into a gorgeous field of sunflowers, snapping family portraits for a friend. The photo shoot was perfect, and the bright yellow flowers were perfectly kissed by the golden sun. As I bent down to take one last photo, I stood up and my necklace caught the handle on my tripod. Snap! My new diamond dropped into the grass below. I stood as still as a statue so I wouldn't lose track of the spot where it had fallen. My friend ran over to help me comb through the blades of grass below. No luck. Her husband lit the ground up with his truck's headlights. Not long afterwards, Jon arrived with a metal detector. The four of us looked and looked for that diamond until we had covered every square inch of the field near where the diamond dropped. I still can't explain how that necklace didn't turn up, but it's clear God had something far more valuable to show me.

The next day I wrestled in my conscience with whether I

should call our insurance agent, also a family friend, and add it to our policy so I could report the loss a few days later. I knew this was wrong. It would have been a lie. It was dishonest and selfish, but it would've been easy to rationalize because of the huge financial implications on our budget. It *was* early in our marriage, after all, and money was tight. I'm sure you wouldn't have done it, but I made that phone call, and I sat under the immense weight of my guilt for the next twenty-four hours. Restless, I found myself at a 5 a.m. spinning class at the gym, my mind a blur. The instructor showed a nature video on the big screen. Time stood still. As my legs pounded the pedals, God illuminated the message He had for me up on that screen. Ocean waves crashed in the video, and drops of sea water dazzled on the screen like thousands of diamonds in the sky. How beautiful! I was reminded that God's Word is like those diamonds, like *my* diamond. It's precious! It's valuable. You can turn it around and around and never exhaust the wonder and beauty it reveals about its Author. God's Word is true, and the Author expects His kiddos to walk out that truth in even the small, everyday moments of our lives. His Word was buried deep within me, and I knew my dishonesty went against the ways of the Lord (see Lev. 19:11, Prov. 12:22, Col. 3:9). Clearly it was time to be honest and admit my wrongdoing. In doing so, I had to trust God's provision for me and that He could handle even circumstances like this one. I didn't need to try to fix the loss in my own strength or grasp onto my material possessions with white knuckles, regardless of the slice of budget pie this necklace represented. Truth is worth more.

As quickly as the class ended, I mustered up the courage to call Jon and tell him what I'd done and about what God had shown me. Yuck! What a horrible feeling. Then, I called our insurance agent and confessed to him, too. I apologized and told him I understood if he needed to drop us as clients. The next moment was shocking. He graciously accepted my apology and told me it was covered. Covered! It would have been covered, he said, from the moment of purchase regardless of when I called. Seriously? I wept. What unmerited grace! What scandal! And how very gospel-like, his response. You see, before you or I even knew to apologize for our sins and wrongdoings, Jesus covered us with grace and forgiveness. It's absurd. No wonder all of Heaven throws a party each time a sinner comes to faith. Stumbling away from that situation with newfound humility, God helped me personally apply the truth of the gospel and the scandal of His grace in a way I'll simply never forget. Meanwhile, I'm pretty sure I will never look at a diamond the same way again.

It wasn't my own wisdom or innate goodness that moved me during the diamond fiasco to do the right thing or to rely on the Lord's strength. That nudge came directly from God, with the Holy Spirit and His Word working together to illuminate truth and push me toward holiness. In the same vein, Exodus 27 paints a picture of the tabernacle, which was the dwelling place of God in the days of the Old Covenant. In the tabernacle, there was to be a lampstand always burning before the Lord, which had to be continually filled with oil to stay aflame. Fast forward to today, under the New Covenant of Jesus, you and I as believers *are* the very dwelling place of God. Like the lampstand, you too must be continually filled with God's light and truth. In turn, you can shine brightly in your everyday life circumstances for the glory of God. You need His Word every day. You're meant to shine.

You are the light of the world-like a city on a hilltop that cannot be hidden. No one lights a lamp and then puts it under a basket. Instead, a lamp is placed on a stand, where it gives light to everyone in the house.

Matthew 5:14-15 (NLT)

D. L. Moody, the great evangelist and publisher, once said, "I prayed for faith and expected it to come out of heaven and strike me like lightning, but it never came. Then one day I read in Romans 10:17 that, 'faith comes by hearing, and hearing by the word of God.' So I started reading my Bible daily, and faith has been growing ever since."[3] The Bible is, therefore, the way God initiates conversation and relationship with you. Everything in the life of a Christian starts here. God is speaking. He's ready to equip you for the day ahead and is patiently waiting to meet with you.

Read your Bible. Seek out the truth. Turn the diamond! Reading God's Word for yourself is how your friendship with God will begin and, increasingly, how it will deepen and grow.

LOVING GOD: PRAYER

James Hudson Taylor, the founder of China Inland Mission, began a protestant evangelistic work in China that resulted in more than 800 missionaries joining his cause for Christ and 18,000 direct conversions to the Christian faith. His strategic vision and immersion into the native Chinese culture has since inspired countless Christian missionaries, including missionary-to-India, Amy Carmichael; Olympic Gold Medalist, Eric Liddell; twentieth-century missionary and martyr, Jim Elliot; founder of Bible Study Fellowship, Audrey Wetherell Johnson; international evangelists, Billy Graham and Luis Palau, and others. Taylor said, "Do not have your concert first, and then tune your instrument afterwards. Begin the day with the Word of God and prayer, and get first of all into harmony with Him."[4] As he so eloquently put it, your prayer life adjoins the time you spend in God's Word to create a slow and steady harmony between you and the Lord.

Slow and steady has a calming ring to it. As I slowed down

from the busy rhythm of life today to enjoy time with God at the writing table, several people came to mind who I needed to call, email, or send a text message to. It took me calming my mind and body to remember I hadn't checked in with those people on some important things happening in their lives. For example, one of my sisters returned from vacation nearly a week ago and had her house on the market while she was away. I've been so busy I simply forgot to ask how the vacation was and if there had been any bites on her house. Knowing the ins and outs of everyday life creates meaningful connection points between friends. After all, life happens daily. Without regular, ongoing communication, relationships grow cold, indifferent, distant, and detached. This is true for any relationship, whether with a spouse, neighbor, friend, or family member, and it's also true in our relationship with God. Intimate relationships require the warmth of conversation and time spent together to thrive. That's what prayer is all about; growing the flame of intimacy with a dear and trusted Friend (John 15:15).

Christianity isn't a religion, it's a relationship. And as we all know, a relationship requires a high commitment to communication. [5]

Kay Arthur

We become more like our earthly friends when we spend time together, aligning our thoughts, patterns of speech, and habits or behaviors with theirs. Every parent knows this to be true. We counsel our kids to choose their friends wisely because we know whatever their friends say and do will most likely be what our kids will end up saying and doing. The same concept applies to you in your walk with Jesus Christ.

You become more Christ-like in your thinking and lifestyle as you immerse yourself into a real relationship with God.

If the Bible is the primary way God speaks to His people today, then prayer is your primary response to God. It's the upward part of the vertical crossbeam, mankind to Maker. Interestingly, as Roxanne Stone of Barna notes, "Prayer is by far the most common spiritual practice among Americans," with 79% of American adults having prayed in the last three months, including 28% of those who claimed "no faith" when asked about their religion.[6] Prayer, as it seems, is as natural to most of us as moving and breathing. For the Christian, prayer is both a great responsibility and privilege. After all, the God of the universe has made a way to approach Him directly through Jesus Christ, His Son - no curtain, no courtyard, no priestly intermediary, no temple sacrifice in tow as was once required in Old Testament times. Unlike any other times in history, you can have direct access today to God the Father without anyone else mediating your conversation with Him apart from Jesus (1 Tim. 2:5). This means God is listening for your voice all the time! Maybe you feel like no one listens to you. Perhaps the opposite is true: you are the big cheese in life and everyone listens to you, but you're not convinced you really even know what you're talking about. In either case, God is all ears and He cares about what *you* have to say.

PRAY CONTINUALLY

How then should you pray, and what should you say when you're talking with God? First of all, you'll want to remember your prayers are not a performance before God or others. Your words don't need to be perfect, polished, flowery, or long-winded, only genuine. You're approaching the throne of grace and an audience of One when you pray, whether alone or in the presence of others, and God's desire is to simply hear the voice of His dear one. What's on your heart and mind?

Share your thoughts with God; He hears you. What are your fears, hurts, and desperations? Share those with God, too. He is with you. What do you admire about God? Is it something He revealed to you in scripture or in the beauty of your surroundings? Praise Him for it. What are you thankful for? Then, offer a quick and heartfelt word of thanks for those things, big or small. Even in the midst of the most troubling circumstances, focusing your heart on what you have to be grateful for can often provide the perspective and strength needed to carry on. Enduring joy, which marks the lives of Christians, goes far deeper than the momentary happiness of worldly pleasures and gains. This is how you can live out the advice Paul gives in 1 Thess. 5:16-18, "Be joyful always; pray continually; give thanks in all circumstances, for this is God's will for you in Christ Jesus." Remember, God has promised that He will work *all things* for the good of those who love Him (Rom. 8:28, *emphasis mine*). His nature is altogether good and He is able, so you can rest in the fact that He's actively working to accomplish His good in your own life and in the world around you. Perhaps, your moments of greatest desperation are providing for you an intimacy with God not otherwise attainable during times of satisfaction and ease, which *is* the greater, enduring good God knows you really need.

> *For we do not have a high priest who is unable to sympathize with our weaknesses, but we have one who has been tempted in every way, just as we are - yet was without sin. Let us then approach the throne of grace with confidence, so that we may receive mercy and find grace to help us in our time of need.*

> Hebrews 4:15-16

JESUS PRAYED

During the days of Jesus' life on earth, he offered up prayers and petitions with loud cries and tears to the one who could save him from death, and he was heard because of his reverent submission. Although he was a Son, he learned obedience from what he suffered and, once made perfect, he became the source of eternal salvation for all who obey him...

Heb. 5:7-9

Jesus walked out the one and only *wholly* holy life. (Say that five times fast!) It makes sense, then, to continually look at Jesus' life as our model, including in the area of prayer. First of all, *did* Jesus regularly pray? If so, *why* did Jesus pray? And if Jesus is Himself God, then why did Jesus *need* to pray? It may be that His prayer life served multiple objectives. Jesus prayed to provide an example for us as His followers (Matt. 6:9). Also, because Jesus was fully God and fully human (Luke 1:35), it would have been completely normal for Jesus the *man* to pray to God as a Jewish believer. Finally, as a member of the Trinity, communication between Father, Son and Holy Spirit has always been an indispensable part of God's relational nature (Gen. 1:26).

If you search the Bible for moments where Jesus prayed, you'll notice just how common it was for Him to talk with the Father. He prayed in the morning (Mark 1:35) and at night (Luke 6:12). He prayed to thank God for His provision (Luke 22:19) and for help in moments of trial and despair (Matt. 26:36-46). He prayed short prayers at times (John 12:28), and for several hours on other occasions (Luke 6:12). Jesus prayed by Himself (Luke 5:16), and He prayed in group settings (Luke 3:21). Jesus prayed for others (Matt. 19:13), and He prayed *with* others (Luke 9:28). He prayed both scripted (Mark 15:34) and impromptu prayers. Jesus prayed knowing that sometimes the outcome of His request to the Father might not be what He asked for, such as the night before the crucifixion when He pleaded with the Father to spare Him from death and separation from His Dad (Luke 22, Matt. 26, Mark 14). Yet, in complete obedience, Jesus next prayed some of the humblest words ever uttered, "Yet I want your will to be done, not mine." (Matt. 26:39 NLT) Jesus' most considerable battle was fought right there on his knees in prayer, that fateful night in the Garden of Gethsemane. He prayed so hard during these hours that, as scripture records, Jesus even sweat drops of blood (Luke 22:44); however, when the time came, Jesus rose from the garden floor, eyes set firmly and resolutely ahead, in full alignment with the good will of God the Father. I've heard it said that every important work in the history of God's Kingdom began in prayer. This was certainly true for the death-defying work of God that soon followed on Calvary's hill.

THE "LORD'S PRAYER"

In addition to the example of how He lived out His life, Jesus also left us with a model prayer, recorded in the gospels. He declared, "This, then, is how you should pray: 'Our Father in heaven, hallowed be your name, your kingdom come, your will be done on earth as it is in heaven. Give us today our daily bread. Forgive us our debts, as we also have forgiven our debtors. And lead us not into temptation, but deliver us from the evil one.'" (Matt. 6:9-13, Lk. 11:2-4) This example prayer of Jesus is thought of by many to be a mini-paraphrase of the gospel itself. And no, it's not the only manner for you and I to pray, in the same way it wasn't the only way Jesus prayed. If you focus, however, on the words Jesus chose for just a moment, there are some beautiful observations and applications to be made that can help shape your own prayer language.

First, God is your Father, beyond comparison by any earthly standards, and He wants to hear from you just like you'd imagine the most adoring daddy would want to hear the voices of his beloved little children. You can approach God as a daughter or son, confidently and intimately, because of what Jesus did on your behalf. You can ask for your Abba Daddy's help and provision because He delights in providing for your needs. You long for your Daddy's name to be "hallowed" on this earth, meaning honored or respected, and for His compassionate, just, and enduring ways to replace all the evil and suffering seen in the world today. God's patience continues every day that this world goes on in its present form, awaiting that next lost soul to come to faith and repentance (2 Pet. 3:9). Meanwhile, the day is near when the reign of God's Kingdom will be ushered in once again on Earth like in Heaven, replacing all we know and see with beauty that will last forever. Oh, what a day that will be!

Continuing on, "give us this day our daily bread…" You can ask God to provide all you need for life today, your spiritual and physical bread. Knowing that God desires only your greatest good, you can ask that He not give you too much or too little and, therefore, protect your heart from being led astray. "And forgive us our debts as we forgive our debtors…" You can beseech the Heavenly Father to forgive your sins, which He says are like debts, each one earning for us a "wage" of death (Rom. 6:23) that must be paid and which can only be forgiven through faith in Jesus Christ, whom He sent. The Creator calls the shots and, according to God, just one inkling of evil, selfishness, hate, or dishonesty is enough to separate you from an all holy God for all time; however, Jesus' payment for sin was made once and for all (Heb. 10:10) and is accompanied by the free gift of God for those who believe, which is everlasting life in the presence of the Lord (Rom. 6:23). What great news! A person rescued from drowning doesn't return to the water to push others under, nor does she brag about how well she gripped onto the life preserver while being towed in, but rather she thanks the person who saved her and goes on to tell others of the rescuer's brave and noble act. Y'all, we've been rescued. Because this is true, you can forgive others when they wrong you, in order to extend God's grace and mercy and to glorify His name.

"And lead us not into temptation, but deliver us from evil..." Finally, like Jesus, you can cry out for God's protection from the snares of the enemy. You simply aren't able to do this life the way Jesus did, because He alone is perfect. Thank heavens, though, that through the power and influence of His Holy Spirit, you can walk in increasing holiness and learn to resist the fiery darts of the enemy seeking your demise. What a prayer. What a confession. What a beautiful way to position yourself in a posture of dependence on God and humble gratitude for His abundant gifts.

A.C.T.S. OF PRAYER

One of my favorite ways to pray, commonly used among various Christian denominations, is following the acronym A. C. T. S. You can think through the components of A. C. T. S. as you enter into conversation with God in this way:

A - Adoration:

What do you most appreciate about God in this moment, or what have you recently learned in scripture about His character (i.e., God's goodness, holiness, faithfulness, strength, wisdom, etc.)? Tell the Lord what you adore or admire about Him. This simple act helps you focus your heart on who God is and recognize the signs of His goodness around every corner.

And they were calling to one another: 'Holy holy, holy is the Lord
Almighty; the whole earth is full of his glory.'

Isaiah 6:3

C - Confession:

After reflecting upon how good, holy, strong, kind, and steady God is, it's easy to recognize all the ways you fall short of Him in your humanness. Confess your mess. Come clean with God about your weaknesses, struggles, failures, and sins. Keep an open and short account with God, and He will forgive you fully and freely.

If we confess our sins, he is faithful and just and will forgive us
our sins and purify us from all unrighteousness.

1 John 1:9

T - Thanksgiving:

In an appropriate posture before the Lord, having practiced adoration and confession, you can now reflect on all the blessings God gives you even though you don't deserve them. A thankful heart is a joyful heart, regardless of one's circumstances; so, reflect on all that is good in your life, and give God thanks.

Be joyful always; pray continually; give thanks in all
circumstances, for this is God's will for you in Christ Jesus.

1 Thessalonians 5:16-18

S - Specific Needs:

The "S" in the A. C. T. S. model technically stands for "supplication," a word you likely don't weave into everyday conversations, but it simply means making requests or asking for what you need. Ask God to meet your needs and the needs of the people in your life and on your mind. He delights in answering the prayers of His people (Prov. 15:8), so ask with expectation, and know He will only answer with what is best for you and for them in light of eternity.

> *If my people who are called by my name humble themselves and pray...then I will hear from heaven...*
>
> 2 Chronicles 7:14 (ESV)

> *And I will do whatever you ask in my name, so that the Father may be glorified in the Son.*
>
> John 14:13

PRAYING SCRIPTURE BACK TO GOD

Praying scripture back to God is another very practical way to align your heart with what He has revealed to be on His. Pro tip: If you practice a regular cadence of memorizing Bible verses with your small batch, you'll find that memorizing scripture will help shape your own vocabulary in prayer to better reflect God's character and will. The early disciples of Jesus did this (see Acts 4:23-31), and Jesus himself did too. After all, whatever the heart is full of, the mouth speaks (Luke 6:45), and Jesus and the disciples certainly made a habit out of saturating their hearts and minds with the Word of God.

Let's say you've written Romans 8:28 on your heart, "And we know that in all things God works for the good of those who love him, who have been called according to his purpose," and the Lord brings this verse to mind. Then, you might pray something like: *Lord, I love you, and I know your plans for me are good. Right now I'm worried and my circumstances are making me feel hopeless. Help me to have confidence that you are working all things for my good and for your glory.*

Here's another way to give this a try. As an example, if you've just spent time studying scripture and searching for the G. P. A. of the text, as we talked about earlier, then you could praise *God* for whatever He's revealed to you about Himself in His Word ("G"). Tell the Lord how you feel about the *people* you've just read about in the Bible ("P"). You might feel surprised or even outraged by their actions or attitudes, or maybe you see a glimmer of yourself in the characters of history. You might be confused by the cultural norms of the day. Talk about your reactions to the text with God, and if something doesn't quite make sense, do some research to better understand any context clues you may be missing. Acknowledge your fears and ask for God's help as you seek to *apply* His truths to your own life ("A"). Think about hand-crafting the foundations of the faith found in this book right into your bible study practices: love God, love others/yourself, and be moved to action.

Our extended family recently hosted a virtual get-together online late one Saturday morning. One of my kids wanted to ask the group if they liked puzzles as much as he did and to show everyone the puzzle he'd been working on, but he struggled to find a way into the conversation. Because so many folks were on the line, there were few natural breaks in the chatter, and it was difficult for him to discern when everyone was done commenting on the previous topic. The problem was every time he tried to pose his question, "So, does anyone else like puzzles?" to the group, he nearly cut someone else off and feared coming across as rude. His polite-meter was on point because, as we all know, changing the subject in the middle of a conversation is impolite. Similarly, I wonder if it's best not to change the subject in the middle of your conversations with God? Truth be told, I think God is delighted to hear anything we have to say, but by praying scripture verses back to God, you can be certain what you're praying is keeping true to your conversation. Take care when you pray, whatever your inspiration, to avoid just going through the motions of mechanical recitation, but rather communicating from the heart with your nearest Friend and confidant.

INTERCEDING IN PRAYER FOR OTHERS

Jesus prayed for many other people along His earthly path, including future believers like you and me (John 17:20). Praying for others is therefore something for you to do, too, and should stem from a place of gratitude that God has provided others for you to journey alongside in life. Frankly, it also helps you to take your mind off your own issues and to refocus on the bigger picture of God's purposes at work around you. Don't miss the opportunity to pray for other people you know and to be encouraged as you watch God at work in their lives in response to your requests.

If you're married, pray for your spouse. This will encourage you to maintain a softened, compassionate heart toward them as time goes on. Pray *with* your spouse whenever possible, which will help you as a couple develop the spiritual intimacy God intends for your marriage.

If you have kids, pray also for your children. They are arrows in your archer's sack, and God has entrusted them to you to shepherd, love, care for, and then send out into this wild world for the sake of the gospel mission. I think the sending process begins in our hearts as parents long before we pack them up for life beyond our home. It's actually the goal all along that their hearts would beat in step with the unimaginable works God has planned for their lives. Therefore, pray for your children's salvation and an adventurous spirit. Pray that the truth of God's Word will be written on their hearts and will serve as an anchor for their souls during their most troubling times. You cannot save your children, and their personal journey of faith must not define yours. Still, your love will point them to God, and your faith can be the winsome magnet He uses in their lives as He draws your children unto Himself at just the right time. The work of parenting God's way is humbling and not for the faint, but of course this, too, is by design and may actually prove more beneficial for your own spiritual growth than theirs.

Pray for others. Pray for your disciples, your spiritual children, as you invite them to also pray for you. Mutual transparency is one of the greatest ways God teaches us through the discipleship process, so don't rob yourself or those you lead of God's glory by adopting a veil of pride. Lift up your neighbors, family members, coworkers, friends, and even your enemies in prayer to the Lord. Because this is *your* unique circle of influence, the reality is you may be the only person approaching the throne of grace today on their behalf.

Pray, finally, for the nations and the unreached people groups of the world. Don't be surprised if God calls you, like He did the first apostles, to leave everything behind for a time to go serve them. Ask for all these things, and watch for God to set each and every answer to your prayers into motion.

Ask and it will be given to you; seek and you will find; knock and the door will be opened to you.

Matthew 7:7

KEY CONCEPTS

- The foundations of the Christian faith include loving God and loving others. You live these out as a disciple of Jesus by studying the Bible, praying, talking about God, cultivating authentic relationships with other believers, and serving others in love.
- The Bible is the primary way God speaks today, and prayer is your primary response back to God.
- G. P. A. Bible study technique: What do you learn about *God* and *people* in the text? What practical *applications* can you make to your own life?
- A. C. T. S. Prayer Method: Adoration, Confession, Thanksgiving, Specific Needs
- Praying scripture back to God aligns your heart with what He has revealed to be on His heart.
- Praying for others helps take your mind off your own challenges and refocuses it on God's purposes at work around you.

DISCUSSION QUESTIONS

1. Have you ever had someone personally walk alongside you in order to help you mature as a Christian? Describe that experience.
2. Do you have a Bible? If so, how are you currently interacting with your Bible? What Bible study techniques or tools have you used to study God's Word? How have those helped you?
3. How has the Holy Spirit helped to illuminate or bring God's Word to life for you? If not yet, why

might this be an important request of God as you begin your quiet time studies?

4. Do you sense yourself becoming more like your friends, including those you only know from a distance, because of the time you spend with them? In what ways have you become more like Jesus over time?

5. What is your current comfort level with prayer, both individually and with others? In what ways would you like to improve your conversations with God or your practice of prayer?

6. Select one verse of scripture from the Bible (either one verse per person or one common verse). Practice personalizing the verse back to God in prayer together now.

chapter six

Loving Others:
fellowship
& evangelism

We double our delight in God as we expand it in the lives of others. [1]

John Piper

Through prayerful study of the Bible, and daily time set aside for communion and consultation with God, you will grow by leaps and bounds in your friendship with God, as well as in wisdom and knowledge. But let's not forget our God is a relational God, existing in three persons Himself, and so it is through worship and fellowship with other believers, as well as inviting those outside of the family of God to meet Jesus, that we will *more fully* know and adore God. Let me put it another way: you are not here primarily for yourself, but for others. If you consider your faith a private matter, wanting only to experience God solo, then you (and all those around you) miss out on so much. The cross was anything but private, and the gospel life is anything but isolated. Therefore, the third and fourth elements of the cross illustration, extending horizontally out from Jesus at the center of our life, are fellowship with other believers, and sharing the gospel with the lost.

LOVING OTHERS: FELLOWSHIP

Technology and travel have created an unprecedented global connectivity in our day, and yet somehow more isolation and loneliness exists today than ever before. In a 2018 study, Barna Group found that the majority of adults in the U. S. have anywhere between two and five close friends, but one in five regularly or often feels lonely.[2] While society-at-large trends away from authentic interpersonal connection, where people interact with vulnerability and look one another in the eye as they communicate face-to-face, each of us as individuals still longs to belong, to be known, and to feel loved.

During the COVID-19 global pandemic of 2020, people around the globe were forced to self-quarantine to reduce the spread of the coronavirus. While under mandate to isolate in their homes, people everywhere looked for creative ways to forge meaningful connections. Life slowed down significantly when the social commitments of modern day existence were suddenly stripped away, and people everywhere discovered how to be "alone together." Townspeople in Europe sang nightly from their balconies. Authors, artists, and musicians shared their gifts with the world using social media. Friends and families engaged in virtual dinners and coffee dates through online meeting platforms, and those who were permitted to do so brought their work home, working alongside their homeschooling children for the first time in their lives. Times like these have put our collective need for one another on full display, humanity rising as busyness subsides. And regardless of the mechanism, the coffeehouse-type experience is still a necessity in our communities today, where neighbors, co-workers, and newfound friends can be seen meeting over steamy mugs and warm conversation. Long live neighborhood cookouts, living room game nights, community gardens, and porch swing romances. The art of human relationship has not been lost.

In a culture of isolation, discipleship relationships are an open door for spiritual transformation.[3]

Barna Group, *State of Discipleship*, 2016

God intends for us to be in relationship with one another through every dip and turn along life's pathway. We buzz right past other people all the time without a second thought as to what their experience today might be like. The people right next to you could be flipping excitedly through pictures of a major life celebration, but just feet away someone else may be shouldering a great burden all alone, wondering if anyone else has ever felt the depths of grief they're experiencing. We are meant to be together through all of this. You see, God's in the business of meeting people right where they are with love, presence, and hope. In doing so, He uses His people to meet one another's needs in both tangible and intangible ways. He is the amazing orchestrator of souls that sovereignly moves us along toward divine encounters with one another, appearing as accidents if we don't pause to see His hand in it all.

They were continually devoting themselves to the apostles' teaching and to fellowship, to the breaking of bread and to prayer.

Acts 2:42 (New American Standard Bible)

Discipleship is relational, and thus life-on-life time within your small batch is as important as any other shared practice. The earliest followers of Jesus were devoted to studying the word of God together, praying, breaking bread, and enjoying one another's fellowship. The original Greek word for fellowship, such as in this verse, is *koinonea* (κοινωνία), and it signifies spiritual community, partnership, sharing, and mutual participation. Fellowship involves a practical relationship lived out between Sundays, meeting so many deep needs we have as humans. Does your heart long for a community where you belong? How about up-close friends who know your real grit and are committed to still walking life out with you? Wouldn't it be great to have someone nearby to help you when the chips are down? This is the fellowship of Christ.

Biblical friendship exists when two or more people, bound together by a common faith in Jesus Christ, pursue him and his kingdom with intentionality and vulnerability. Rather than serving as an end in itself, biblical friendship serves primarily to bring glory to Christ, who brought us into friendship with the Father. It is indispensable to the work of the gospel in the earth, and an essential element of what God created us for. [4]

Jonathan Holmes

The majority of our closest friendships in life have been with disciples and other friends who share a passion for Jesus. Our faith network literally kept us moving forward when the going got tough. For example, many years ago, after selling our vehicle to save up for the expenses of delivering a baby, we were given a car by a fellow believer. Through prayer, God's timing was made clear to us to sell Jon's beloved, shiny red truck; meanwhile, He had placed it on the heart of a dear friend to give their car away to us! A bit farther down the road, we had the blessing of passing our "Jesus Car" along to someone else in need once we'd saved up enough to afford another vehicle. That's how God works. God meets our needs through community, and He entrusts us to steward all we've been given as if doing so on His behalf.

Companionship (is) between people who (are) doing something together - hunting, studying, painting, or what you will...Friends will still be doing something together, but something more inward, less widely shared, and less easily defined; still hunters, but of some immaterial quarry; still collaborating, but in some work the world does not, or not yet, take account of; still traveling companions, but on a different kind of journey.[5]

C.S. Lewis

The blessings of community extend beyond practical needs alone. Through the years, our faith family also held us up in prayer when life's burdens were too heavy to bear. They listened as we wrestled through marriage struggles, work challenges, and parenting worries. They pressed in when pain came crashing in like a hurricane, unafraid and unwavering in their friendship. There have been board games, big "extended family" dinners, date nights, and living room worship sessions. But this fellowship goes beyond a simple companionship. It's something much deeper. Our disciples and faith family know the real Sully family. They are traveling companions on an eternal journey, and we feel forever connected with them through Jesus. Your small batch relationships will similarly live on, long beyond the time of organized, weekly discipleship gatherings, as long as you keep rolling out the welcome mat for others to come inside.

VULNERABILITY

Vulnerability sounds like truth and feels like courage. Truth and courage aren't always comfortable, but they're never weakness.[6]

Brené Brown

When you're willing to be vulnerable with others regarding the struggles you're going through, then the weight of proving and comparing yourself to others falls away. When you're free from self-imposed expectations of perfection, you're able to be there for others as they wade through their own challenges. Vulnerability enables authenticity and helps to establish buy-in and trust. This is how you should experience the local church and your small batch discipleship community, all imperfect, needing Jesus, and leaning in to point one another toward God.

C. S. Lewis described three ways humanity goes astray in his book, *Mere Christianity*: 1) letting our fleshly desires interfere with our morality; 2) drifting apart from one another; and 3) forgetting about the salvation of mankind through Jesus. The alternative, Lewis shares, would be: 1) inner harmony; 2) harmony between individuals, and 3) participation in the greater purposes of our lives in relation to God.[7] Looking around, it seems pretty clear these concerns still hold true today. Harmony doesn't often characterize our hustle and flow lifestyles. And sadly, even in Christian circles we often fall prey to the rumblings of pride, envy, conflict, and divisiveness. Lewis uses the metaphor of an orchestra to illustrate the constant balancing act between an individual, larger society, and God. Each instrument must be in tune, come in at the right time, and play the same musical score in harmony with all the other instruments. What would happen, though, if one instrument wasn't in good working condition or was constantly playing over all the others? What if, collectively, the orchestra played a different song than the conductor directed? The end result would be exactly what C.S. Lewis described.

Can you see how this compares so well to our Christian walk? Each of us has to stay in tune with Christ. If not, we won't be in sync with God about the direction of our lives. Furthermore, we'll be bumping into one another left and right, jumping in at all the wrong times, and hindering the world from hearing the beauty of the Conductor's masterpiece.

In his book, *Tally Ho the Fox*, Herb Hodges describes a pack of fox hounds.[8] Left to their own devices, they scratch and snarl and fight. But when a fox runs by, when the horn is blown, they set off in unison fixed on the fox. Running side-by-side, they actually spur one another along. The pack is stronger together. They run faster and farther alongside one another than they could ever run on their own. All the issues and preoccupations that once caused conflict among them simply fade into distant memories. What would happen if we as the Church were truly tracking together in the footsteps of Jesus?

Satan's strategy is always to divide and conquer. God, on the other hand, intends for us to serve one another as true companions and teammates. As a matter of fact, the Bible describes each follower of Christ as a living stone (1 Pet. 2:4-8) in the Church He's still building today. Each living stone is meant to maintain its individuality but, meanwhile, to forego isolation and independence as a part of the larger whole. Every stone lends its ability to carry weight and plays a vital role in relation to all the other stones in the building. It's a continuation of the Hebrew word *echad* seen throughout the Old Testament, which conveys a collective sense of oneness

(Deut. 6:4, Jer. 32:38-40), a rich unity that God is calling His people into, each one part of the greater whole. You and I are indeed a special part of a larger body, the Church, and scripture is subsequently filled with "one another" verses that explain how we can interact with harmony, unity, and shared purpose. Sometimes, though, it feels as though we're more like porcupines in the snow, longing to huddle together for warmth, but instead poking and needling each other to death the closer we get. We are fingers cold inside their glove, needing to drop our dividers and embrace the beauty of togetherness. It's time we chose community over competition.

> *...And I pray that you, being rooted and established in love, may have power, together with all the Lord's holy people, to grasp how wide and long and high and deep is the love of Christ, and to know this love that surpasses knowledge—that you may be filled to the measure of all the fullness of God.*

Ephesians 3:17-19

Paul Harvey, famed radio newscaster always said, "And now, the rest of the story…" Small batch relationships, where faith can be multiplied among friends, *are* the rest of the story so many of us as Christians have been missing. Think about it. When you connect in real community with other believers, vulnerably sharing the struggles and joys you're experiencing in life, you're then able to see all the ways God shows up in these circumstances, which in turn helps your love and trust for God to grow. You can multiply the truth He has shown you in His Word by sharing it with someone else. You can meet the practical needs of your neighbors with a spirit of true generosity. In the small batch, you can laugh and cry together and encourage a mutual, passionate pursuit of Jesus. In this togetherness, the sweet spot where revelational and relational theology come together, learning *and* loving, you become the hands and feet of Jesus to your brothers and sisters in Christ. God Himself is more fully known and His compassion is put on display through real Christian fellowship. Don't go it alone, believer. God has placed others all around you for a reason.

LOVING OTHERS: EVANGELISM

> *Now after John was arrested, Jesus came into Galilee, proclaiming the gospel of God, and saying, 'The time is fulfilled, and the kingdom of God is at hand; repent and believe in the gospel.'*

Mark 1:14-15 (ESV)

Our final foundational element of the Christian life is evangelism, simply meaning loving others by sharing the good news of Jesus Christ with them. Literally translated, evangelism means "good news-ing" others. If you know and love Jesus, then at some point along life's journey someone else shared the good news of the gospel with you. Somehow, someway, that person explained how you needed God to forgive your imperfections, just like them, and that you could never earn God's forgiveness on your own. While you were busy adding sins to your rap sheet and feverishly pursuing your own purposes, they cared enough to reach out to you that you might understand God's greater purposes for your life and enjoy Him for all eternity. Thank goodness they did.

Just one sinful offense on the scorecard of life is enough to separate you and me from an all holy God, but God made a way. He planned a solution to this problem of ours before we even breathed our first breath. From the very beginning, knowing how history would unfold, God planned a Savior to rescue His people from their own sins. At just the right moment in history, Jesus Christ stepped down into His own creation to make it happen.

THE GREAT RESCUE

Jesus Christ, God in the flesh, left the perfection and glory of His heavenly kingdom, entered into this broken world, wrapped himself in humanity, lived the one and only perfect life ever lived, died a sinner's death on a cross, was buried, rested in a tomb for three days, and then rose back to life with victory over death. Many people witnessed this, and the resurrected Jesus proclaimed that all who believe in Him with their whole hearts and lives will also receive from Him life beyond the grave, everlasting life *with* God. This is the good news of the gospel of Jesus Christ. All of Heaven awaited this moment, when the mystery of God finally unfolded, and here it was: the rescue of mankind. We see God's promise of rescue gracing every story of scripture, of course, all the way back to sin's first heartbreak in the garden with Adam and Eve. You've heard the famous line spoken in 1970 by Apollo 13 astronaut, James Lovell, "Uh, Houston, we've had a problem."[9] God's words in Genesis chapter three sounded something more like this, "People, we have a problem. But I have the answer. I love you, and I will send a Rescuer to bring you back to me. He is coming, and He will fix this."

The great Rescuer offers the same promise to you today. Your proper response to the gospel, according to Jesus, is to repent and believe, meaning to turn away from your own way of doing things and to reorient your heart toward God. Surrender to God. Rest your whole self in Jesus alone. Like sitting back trustingly in a chair, allow Him to bear your full weight. Faith is not pointing to the chair and talking about how trusty it is and how it *could* hold you up. Faith is sitting in it, resting in it, even lifting your feet off the ground. Faith is in the surrender, and in the surrender, you receive acceptance,

peace with God, adoption into God's family, and life forever
with the One who loves you best and most. Is this kind of
surrender and acceptance a chapter in your life story yet? If
not, open up to God in prayer. Confess your need to Him and
simply rest in Jesus.

WE'RE WIRED FOR PRAISE

Once rescue unfolds in your life, your heart will naturally
light on fire to share the love and peace you've found in God
with others. That's what praise looks like, when you are so lit
up inside about someone or something that you just can't help
but talk about them. I think this is why God calls His kiddos to
praise Him throughout the Bible. Have you ever wondered
about that before? Honestly, have you ever asked yourself
whether it's sort of vain that God calls people to praise Him? I
know I have. It's not a vain request in reality, though, because
God knows we're wired to give a good shout-out when it's
deserved.

Picture for a moment the best meal you've ever had. What
was it? It was *soooo* good, right? Maybe it was the best steak in
the city (or your favorite tofu bowl) and you just couldn't rest
until you told somebody else about it. You *had* to do this. Then
and only then, would you feel fully satisfied. Well, this is true
with your faith, as well. When you're head over heels in love
with God, you just have to tell somebody. If you are really
convinced the truth of God is actually true, then isn't this the
very most important thing you have to offer other people
anyhow? The good news of the gospel should change everything, and that's why becoming comfortable talking about
God with others is an important part of the discipleship
process. Consider this: if you aren't talking about God,
why not?

GOD-CONVERSATIONS

I remember the first time I was part of a God-conversation that resulted in a salvation decision. Jessica, a high school student in the discipleship small group I led at our local church, handed out groceries with me at a food pantry in the city. She and I were assigned to the evangelism station, where recipients of groceries were offered the opportunity to hear the good news of the gospel and receive prayer with a believing volunteer. The people in line for groceries had all been through this before, so we really didn't expect much to happen. Not to mention, there was no official test or training for this; we were just told to give it a go. Yikes! Awkwardly, Jessica and I fumbled our way through sharing the gospel message with one woman. She pressed in. The conversation continued. To our amazement, she reached out, held our hands with tears and a burdened heart, and prayed to receive and follow Jesus Christ. The woman's name was Christian. (Seriously!)

Jessica and I played a special but small part along Christian's spiritual journey, as another group of believers stepped in over the days that followed to help her deepen her relationship with God and continued to meet her physical needs. Looking back, I realize I never told Jessica how my insides were doing somersaults of excitement during all of this, because I was afraid she'd think less of me for never having led someone to Jesus before. As the leader of this gospel outing, I played it cool, which was *so* not cool. Correct me if I'm wrong, but I think many of us feel this way. Maybe you can relate. Perhaps you've been a believer for years, or even a spiritual influencer, but have never had the privilege of leading someone else to faith in Jesus. Please don't feel one iota of shame over this or accept the enemy's lie that you have to hide it like a dirty secret, like I did with Jessica. God has countless opportunities for God-conversations already marked out for you, and you never know at which step along someone else's faith journey

God will use you. Friends, let's be humble and ready so each of us can be used by God for eternal moments like these, whether planting, watering, or bringing the harvest.

Oftentimes people say they don't feel "gifted" in evangelism (like 99% of us), so they think gospel-sharing is for someone else to do who's had more training, has a different personality style, is more extroverted, or more courageous. The truth is, though, you may be the only Christian person God ever aligns with the people you interact with each day. What's more, those lucky few folks who actually *do* feel gifted in this area could never be in every conversation and every location where there's a need for God. And remember, the Great Commission is a command for all of us individually and collectively ("all y'all"); therefore, sharing the good news of the gospel of Jesus Christ is a key facet of being and making disciples of Christ.

When I first became a believer, I learned so much from older, wiser Christians. I'm thankful for their patience and influence in my faith life. Seriously, because I asked some ridiculous questions and made plenty of stupid statements as I wrestled through my own doubt and misunderstandings. I felt safe, though, to do that wrestling within the small batch moments of my life. I still do. But, I also remember times when others made me feel embarrassed about my excitement for the Lord and encouraged me to temper my enthusiasm to avoid coming across too "over the top." I wondered why people who claimed to adore Jesus would discourage me from sharing my excitement about God's grace with others. I wondered if they really believed what they claimed to believe about Jesus. Had they forgotten what a difference the love of God had made in their lives? Is this tempering of excitement what Jesus would want for His Church, or is it more that those who have walked with Jesus for a while need a fresh infusion of enthusiasm and zeal that new believers bring? I'm guessing it's the latter and that this tendency should point us toward a reverse mentorship, of sorts, in our discipleship circles, in addition to the traditional approach. Discipleship, after all, is a two-way street. For now, let's put a pin in the mentorship idea and circle back to it in the next section on leadership.

Young and old, veteran and new, Jesus wants all of us. God saved His people to love and enjoy forever. Let me remind you of something, though. If this were all He wanted with us, again don't you think He would have swooped us up long ago to be with Him in Heaven? Yet He didn't. He left you and me here on this earth for a purpose. As believers, God's Holy Spirit is with us and inside of us. It's as if Jesus has returned to the earth in the form of each one of us. According to scrip-ture, we are His "holy temple" in the flesh. So, for as long as God intends, you and I are here to be His very presence and truth in the lives of all the people He has placed around us. He surely could have done it much better Himself by just showing up…poof! But He didn't go that route. Maybe an imperfect vessel like you or me is the best way to call another imperfect person to this great adventure of grace. Somehow then, sharing your faith with other people becomes a very logical next step.

I was asked by a pastor recently, "What do you say to the people who just aren't comfortable doing that?" What about those who just want to keep visiting their neighborhood coffee shop for years in hopes of cultivating a rich, personal relation-ship with their favorite barista long before they ever talk to them about Jesus? There are some serious concerns with that approach, though. First, what if next time you visit your favorite java stop, or any other place of business for that matter, your favorite server isn't there anymore? What if today was actually their last day, on the job or even on this earth? What if, instead, you're missing out on years of something far better than casual chit chat, if you had only gotten around to a more meaningful spiritual conversation earlier?

Jesus spoke plainly about the need to repent and turn your

heart toward God; meanwhile, sharing the message of repentance that leads to salvation with other people is the one thing that Christians are most afraid of doing. Am I right? It's scary. You're afraid of what others might say or if they'll laugh at you. You worry they'll ask a question you aren't prepared to answer. When a conversation teeters on the spiritual, your heart races, your mind goes blank, and you heap guilt upon yourself while unearthing some tidy way to back out of the situation at hand. You drop the proverbial spiritual ball out of fear, forgetting though that Jesus-followers aren't meant to have every answer to every question someone might ask. Neither are you responsible for others' reactions to God's love offering. You are instructed, rather, to always be prepared to talk about the reason for your hope, in your own special way, with gentleness and respect (1 Pet. 3:15). The mystery of a moment like this is part of God's plan. *You* are the way God chooses to tell them, flawed and wrestling through a messy faith yourself. God invites *you* into the life-changing work He is doing, and it's for your good that you partner with Him in it. Jesus says when you confess Him before others, He will confess you before the Father (Matt. 10:32).

Evangelism doesn't have to be intimidating. What if you took the pressure off of yourself for delivering a theologically spotless sermon when you talk to other people about God, and just open your mouth to swap stories with them? It can be as natural as that. Have you ever watched a movie preview? A preview doesn't show you the whole movie, but the idea is you get to see just enough of the storyline to want to see the whole thing. You're drawn back to the theater for more. Your life is kind of like that movie trailer, giving people a glimpse of Jesus in your own special way. Your words and actions tell the story of God's work in your life, and it's an important part of the overall storyline of redemption. Based on what they see in you, other people will decide whether they want more of Jesus.

STORYTELLERS

As humans, we're all individually and culturally inclined toward storytelling. If you've had a personal encounter with God, then you have a spiritually valuable truth to share. Maybe yours is one of those glorious salvation stories where God reached down and pulled you from darkness and despair. Tell that story every chance you get, knowing your message might very well light up someone else's night sky. Alternatively, if your life has been spent under the wing of the Almighty, protected from what might have been if you were otherwise left to your own devices, then God has undoubtedly carried you through difficult times and provided you with comfort and encouragement along your way. Tell that story! Whatever your walk with Jesus has looked like, it's very likely God will align your path with someone else who needs to hear exactly what *you* have to share. It's what He does.

What is your faith story? If you can't articulate it yet, or if you need to reflect more on where you're currently at along your faith journey before you put it into words, I'd encourage you to ask yourself the following questions.

1. What did my life look like before God?
2. How did I first encounter Jesus, and what was that experience like for me?
3. What has life looked like since following Jesus?
4. If I have been a Christian for as long as I can remember, then how has God carried me through a difficult time in my life? Or, how is He carrying me through a season of heartache or brokenness today?

Practice talking through your faith story in the safety of your small batch relationships. Once you're comfortable with the story you have to tell, think about how you might enter into a faith-based conversation with someone else.

This is easier than you might think. First of all, you need to get yourself into a mindset of openness to personal interactions. Devices down, eyes up, be looking for opportunities to pause; try not to see others as an interruption to your day. Wherever you are going, put your spiritual antennae up and look for the people God has placed all around you. How might you serve them in love? How can you make room for them in your life by offering up your full attention and presence? For example, when you eat at a restaurant, try asking your waiter or waitress something like this: *We are about to pray for our food. Is there anything we can pray for you about today?* Don't worry if it feels like a new muscle to flex. Take my word for it. Try this out a couple of times, and you'll start feeling more comfortable. You might be surprised, actually, to see how often people will open up to you when you ask a question like this. Greg Holder, pastor of The Crossing church in St. Louis, said it this way, "When others hear you pray their name out loud, it echoes long after the 'amen.'"[10]

I believe, in reality, people everywhere are in need of a giant dose of compassion and are longing for someone else to reach out, to see them right where there are. Who knows? Maybe God has even equipped you to meet their practical needs yourself. Be ready to love others as Jesus would. Little moments like these could mean big things for the Kingdom.

MEET EMILY

One sunny morning, Emily and a group of fellow disciples met for coffee, which stretched into lunch, at a corner cafe in Memphis. They asked the server, "We are about to pray for our food. Is there anything we can pray for you about today?" Right then and there, the server invited Emily and her friends to pray hand-in-hand with her for a serious personal need. Just

10 minutes later, another waitress from inside the cafe hurried out to their table and exclaimed, "I heard you prayed with my coworker, and I really need you to pray for me, too!" Isn't that amazing? One simple, little invitation opened the door for God to love on those two women in just the way they needed that day.

Revelation 12:11 imparts, "They overcame him by the blood of the Lamb and by the word of their testimony; they did not love their lives so much as to shrink from death." You may find this passage encouraging when it comes to sharing your faith story with others. "They" in this verse refers to believers in Christ, and the "him" they conquered is our enemy, Satan. How did they do it? By the blood of the Lamb, Jesus Christ, and by the word of their own stories. According to this Bible verse, both of these tools are equally powerful in our conversations with the lost for the sake of the Kingdom of God: the truth about Jesus' death on the cross and His resurrection, and our very own rescue stories. Notice also how the verse says they didn't love their own lives so much that they would shrink back from death.

I'm not sure where you call home. If you live in a culture where your personal safety or your place in society is put at risk by confessing the name of Jesus Christ, then Revelation 12:11 speaks personally to you about the power of a wise confession in defeating the ultimate opponent. My prayers are with you now for strength, discernment, and boldness for the cause of Christ. For the rest of us, we don't often face immediate death or danger for our confession, but more likely a threat to our pride. May we, too, boldly share the gospel and our own stories with others, and remember as we do what Cinderella says: "Have courage, and be kind."[11]

UNLIKELY COFFEEHOUSE ENCOUNTER

My husband, Jon, was overseas years ago in a place

closed to the gospel, a country where it is still illegal to speak openly about Jesus. One afternoon, Jon walked into a busy coffee shop right in the middle of the city. He hadn't run into anyone so far that day who spoke English, and neither did he speak the local language. Longing to add to our traveler's collection, Jon was on the hunt for a certain coffee mug. As he tried to describe the desired souvenir with his hands, sprinkling in a few English words here and there out of habit, the barista responded using perfect English, "Oh, yeah. We have those right over here. Follow me." The two proceeded to a rack of mugs, picking out the exact one Jon was hoping for. He asked the barista where he'd learned to speak English like that. The worker explained he had been an exchange student in the States a few months back. Jon asked if anyone had ever shared the gospel of Jesus Christ with him during the months he was in the U.S. The coffee shop worker said, "No, but I wish you'd tell me right now." Then, he immediately took off his apron, laid it on the counter, and told his coworkers he was taking his break. Jon, a traveling buddy, and this man each pulled a chair up to the closest table and talked all the way through the gospel message. The barista called another coworker over to join the conversation, explaining to Jon and his companion that they'd been discussing Christianity over the past few days. Afterwards, the barista said he wanted to join them and to follow Christ. How incredible! A connection was made right away with local believers who could get to know this young man and disciple him in his newfound faith.

In reality, this moment was the mountain peak that dozens of smaller moments had been leading up to. God prepared the way, spun the globe, and shepherded His people into this conversation. Like Esther in the Old Testament, I think each of their life stories had been written every moment leading up to this one for "such a time as this" (Esther 4:14). This is how our God works. It's incredible. And, if we're open to it, He can use each one of us in this same personal, Kingdom-centered way.

GOD, MAN, CHRIST, RESPONSE

Back to you. Imagine you set out today with your spiritual antennae up. You're ready to love on others. You're ready to give people your full presence, wherever the day takes you. You're feeling likely to strike up some conversations with other people and are secretly hoping for a chance to brag about God's goodness in one or two of them. If you find your way into a conversation about the Lord, what will you say? Let's think through it together. It may help you feel more prepared to have un-weird conversations about Jesus if you practice regularly retelling yourself the good news of the gospel; or even better, if you practice with a friend. While practice doesn't necessarily make perfect, despite how the saying goes, it does make whatever you practice more permanent. So, if you're ready to give it a try, one way to walk through the gospel is this: *God, Mankind, Christ, Response.*

First, **God**. God is the Creator and Sustainer of everything we see and all that we know. He has no beginning but instead began everything (Gen. 1:1). He is all powerful, all knowing, and present everywhere. God is completely good, kind, and holy, and He created us to be a reflection of Himself and to enjoy a loving relationship with Him.

Next, **Mankind**. We were created for a relationship with God, but unlike God, we are not completely good, kind, or holy. We sometimes lie, steal, gossip, envy one another, and hurt others. We fail to put God on the throne of our lives or to worship Him in the way He deserves, often worshipping ourselves instead. We have gone our own way and declared independence from Him. Assuming we're the captains of our own ships, we routinely set sail in the direction of our own selfish satisfaction. Unfortunately, just one of these less-than-holy things is enough to separate us from God with a chasm we could never crawl, scratch, or climb our own way across. This is a serious problem. Knowing how our heart choices would unfold, God had a plan from the very beginning to fix it.

Enter **Christ**. God loves us so much that He pursued us through the person of Jesus Christ. Jesus, God's own Son, left heaven's throne on high, entered into His own creation, and put on human flesh in order to rescue us. He lived the one and only perfect life we couldn't live. He succeeded in every area where we've failed. He died the death you and I deserved to die because of our rebellion. He was crucified in your place and mine, separated from God, and was treated the way we deserve so that, in life and eternity, we will be treated by God the way He deserves. He was buried and then rose from the dead to defeat death once and for all. God said Jesus' sacrificial death was enough to serve as a payment for us.

What should our **Response** to all this be, then? Jesus said, "Repent and believe" (Mark 1:15, Luke 24:47). Therefore, if you trust Him in all He has done for you and abandon your way of doing life for His way, then you will get to be with Jesus for all eternity and His benefits will be yours forever. Confess your need for Jesus by talking with God in prayer. Accept the gift of His forgiveness. God said, "This is my Son whom I love, with him I am well pleased. Listen to him!" (Matt. 17:5) Have you rested the full weight of your faith in Jesus Christ? Faith involves action. Sit in the chair. Trust in Jesus. The free gift of God awaits you.

I've heard the gospel likened to a traffic story. Imagine you're in a long line of traffic on the highway, cars dead stopped across multiple lanes of traffic. You've been sitting in this line for far too long, and you're trying desperately to keep road rage at bay while you avoid looking at your watch, because you know you're going to be late if you sit there any longer. Up ahead the left lane is closed and you'll eventually have to merge over into the right lane, but of course nearly everyone else is merging now because of the traffic. Then along comes *that* guy. You know the guy. He drives past all the other cars that have been patiently waiting so long, and he expects to skip the line and weave in ahead of everyone else. The nerve! Then, the unimaginable happens. Somebody actually waves him in! Unbelievable. In all his audacity, it's like he thinks he's better than everyone else and deserves a fast-pass to the front of the line. Now, pause a minute with me and pull up from this scene, because this is the gospel. *You* are that guy. Somebody gave you the pass. The nerve! You didn't deserve one bit of it, driving along in life according to your own rules like you owned the road, but God waved you in. It's scandalous! This is grace.

Retell the gospel to yourself again and again until the relentless, scandalous, gracious love of God overwhelms you from the inside out. Then, practice sharing the audacious truth of the gospel out loud with your small batch crew. *God, Man, Christ, Response.* You tell them, then they tell you. Offer encouragement to one another as you do this. Use your own words. Make the truths of God come to life in your conversations.

Let's be honest, Christians sometimes come across as weird or socially awkward with others. If this sounds familiar to you, don't sweat it. Embrace your own awkwardness. The truths of God are counter-cultural anyhow. Don't clean it up, just talk about God in your own special way. On the other hand, if you have a natural way with words, then use your own fabulous style to tell others what you've found to be true about God, too. Whatever your conversational gifting, make the true story of Jesus Christ and your own faith story fit into your everyday conversations whenever the Spirit of God makes a way. As you enter into a conversation with someone, ask the Holy Spirit what part of your story the person you're talking with needs to hear most. Then, grounded in love, set the words free.

> *For, everyone who calls upon the name of the Lord will be saved. How, then, can they call on the one they have not believed in? And how can they believe in the one of whom they have not heard? And how can they hear without someone preaching to them? And how can they preach unless they are sent? As it is written, 'How beautiful are the feet of those who bring good news!'*
>
> Romans 10:13-15

ONE VERSE EVANGELISM

In addition to sharing your own faith story, or the *God, Man, Christ, Response* gospel message, you can also use one simple scripture verse to tell God's story. In the ESV, Romans 6:23 teaches, "For the wages of sin is death, but the free gift of God is eternal life in Christ Jesus our Lord." Compare and contrast the two sides of that truth, maybe even on a napkin or the back of a receipt. Great things are always happening on the backs of napkins! On one side, write the words "wages," "sin," and "death." In another column to the right, write, "free gift," "of God," and "eternal life." Explain that a wage is something you earn, and that, according to God, what we've earned through our own sin is death. It may be helpful to explain to the other person that sin is defined as anything less than perfection, and you might include some common examples that everyone struggles with. This is the ugly truth of our condition. We need help. But wait, there's more! The other side of this verse is the good news of the gospel. Ask the other person to describe a gift. A gift is something you haven't earned. It's free and simply received from the giver. God's free gift to us is eternal life with Him, and the way to receive it is by believing in His Son, Jesus Christ, and what He has done for us on the cross. Invite the other person to turn away from their old way of doing life and toward God and His way, believing in Jesus and beginning an everlasting relationship with Him today through faith.

EMPATHIC LISTENING

I want to share one final idea with you as you practice sharing the good news of Christ's love with others, perhaps my favorite method of evangelism: listening to other people's stories with an ear for a bridge to the gospel. The bridge could be any connection between someone's greatest need or longing in life and how God alone can meet that need.

MEET IMANI

Early one morning, Imani set her bag down a few feet away from another woman and pulled up a neighboring lounge chair at the pool. Imani looked over and wondered if she should try to strike up a conversation with this woman. Imani's spiritual antennae were up, but what if the woman just wanted to be left alone? It was odd, after all, that this other lady was all alone on a pool deck, hours before normal sunbathing hours. On top of that, the two of them looked nothing alike and were clearly separated by a few decades, so there was no easy connection to make based on similarity. Her heart aflutter, Imani rolled over and struck up a conversation. She asked the woman if there was anything going on in her life that she might allow a random stranger like her to talk and pray with her about. In hindsight, Imani knew she could have easily laughed at her and asked her not to bother her while she relaxed poolside. That isn't what happened, though. Instead, the woman actually shared with Imani that her marriage was falling apart and that she longed for restoration with her husband. Imani didn't jump into the conversation flinging out scripture verses or a prepared script. She really listened. The woman openly shared. Again, this conversation was proof that people everywhere are craving moments just like this. And as Imani listened, God slowly gave her just the right words to say in return. Imani encouraged her new friend that God alone brings true peace and restoration, that He lavishes us with His love and helps us let others off the hook for meeting our deepest needs in ways they will never be able to do. She gently explained that Jesus brings reconciliation between us and the God who adores us. And finally, she shared how God gives us a ministry of reconciliation in this world on His behalf (2 Cor. 5:11). What a God we serve!

This poolside conversation was an unlikely yet sweet exchange. What a moment God created there, and how loving it was that God used Imani, a flawed and messy vessel of His grace, to provide the encouragement another person's heart most needed that day. Imani left that moment more in love with God, who truly meets us where we are, and with a heart more tender toward others and what they might be going through.

When you begin to ask other people to share their stories with you, you should approach them with genuine curiosity rather than your own agenda. Ask people about themselves. Really listen to what they have to say. Stretch your empathy muscles. Quiet the inner monologue inside your head and see if you might learn something interesting from them before sharing your own thoughts and stories. If you're wondering where to start, consider asking others what it was like for them growing up, or what big things they are struggling with most in life right now. Obviously, those are big questions. You could also start by simply asking them what they're reading or the latest movie they've watched. As you listen to what's on their minds, you can eventually share good things about the God who's on yours.

We all need God. Jesus Christ *is* the bridge to experiencing reconciliation, peace, love, forgiveness, healing, joy, adventure, and whatever else our hearts long for in this life. Jesus alone can fill the God-sized hole in our hearts that we try to fill with so many other things. And once we turn and let Him in, He promises never to leave or forsake us. Somebody you'll meet today probably needs to hear that.

MEET ELIANA

Eliana joined Morgan and a few fellow disciples to venture out at midnight on Black Friday, years ago when people still lined up in the early morning hours to snag the best shopping deals from their favorite retailers. The group toted along wagons of hot cocoa to hand out to cold shoppers, hoping for an opportunity to share the real "deal" truly worth being out in the cold at this obscene hour. A new believer herself, Eliana felt intimidated to share her faith that night with anyone they met because of her own language barrier. However, before everything was said and done, and at the encouragement of her sweet discipler, Eliana ended up with an opportunity to share the gospel in her native tongue with several shoppers and to eventually lead one of those individuals to faith in Jesus in the parking lot. Had Eliana not been there that night or been brave enough to jump into a gospel conversation, that person's eternity might still hang in the balance today.

Has God ever dropped you on the other side of your comfort zone for the sake of a spiritual conversation? Too many times, in moments like these, I've surrendered to the fear of rejection only to find that God patiently provided yet another opportunity again soon afterwards. And then there was the time when I found myself turning around in traffic toward a moment the Holy Spirit wouldn't let me miss.

SPIRITUAL U-TURN

It was early evening, and I was shopping for tripods at a photography store. The staff were helping other people as I browsed, when suddenly the store cleared out. All the workers but one went back into the storage area of the building. The other customers exited through the front door. There was just one clerk and I left in the little showroom. It was honestly a bit strange. We talked about photography, I demoed a few tripods, and then I felt my heartbeat quicken. I knew I was supposed to share the gospel with this person. There was no mistaking it, but I was afraid, so I paid for my stuff and quickly left. As I drove away, I felt such conviction I could hardly breathe, much less continue driving. I made a quick u-turn across traffic (which I don't advise) and drove back to the store as quickly as I could. As I pulled up, the clerk met me at the door and walked outside. That seemed strange, too. I wondered what was happening. Apparently the clerk had given me the tripod box and whatever else I had bought, but he forgot to put the tripod into my bag. So, there we stood, outside the store on a quiet sidewalk. I started talking and explained to him how God had made me turn around to share His love with him. I'm sure my words weren't perfect and I honestly can't even remember what was said as we spoke. It wasn't a moment leading into a salvation prayer, at least to my knowledge, but I felt such overwhelming peace and joy having heard God correctly and obeying God by sharing my faith. Most likely I'll never know the spiritual significance of this moment for the store clerk, but it was a moment I'll never forget. I was fully God's in this moment, and I knew I wouldn't feel quite as timid the next time I sensed the gentle whisper of the Spirit of God nudging me to speak on His behalf. Isn't it marvelous how God uses people like you and me in moments like this? Surely it's for our good as much as anyone else's.

One of the roles of the Holy Spirit is to prepare the soil of people's hearts to hear and respond to the Word of God. This is the reason you don't have to be afraid to jump into spiritual conversations. You haven't arrived first. He is already there! He has aligned your path with the path of that other person, and it's not by accident. Talk with them. If the person is a "person of peace" and presses into your conversation, as the Bible describes in Luke chapter 10, you'll know it. That's when things will get really interesting. If not, then give yourself the freedom to move on about your day knowing that you faithfully flung seeds of the gospel as you were going along. God will carry the weight of responsibility for the planting, watering, and harvesting of those seeds of truth (1 Cor. 3:6-7).

Sometimes...fear does not subside and...one must choose to do it afraid. [12]

Elisabeth Elliot

Great works of God often begin in seemingly insignificant conversations, un-sparkly acts of service, on napkin scribbles, in photography stores, and in small batch relationships. Jill Briscoe said it this way, "The mission field's between your own two feet at any given time." [13] So, be relational with people. Serve others in practical ways with love. Be sure to set time aside to practice articulating the gospel with a friend or loved one, or in your small batch discipleship or faith community, and then watch for opportunities today and every day where you can share what you *already* know about God's love with someone else. If you're afraid, then "go in" afraid, tummy butterflies in tow. Trust God to give you the words to say, and set the words free.

The Navigators, an international discipleship organization, uses a wheel to illustrate the Christian life.[14] The same four foundations (i.e., crossbeams) we've studied together are pictured as four spokes on a wheel, with Jesus as the hub at the center. When life gets spinning around, which I'm sure we'd all agree that it does, you really don't notice the spokes anymore, which are radiating out from the hub to the edges of the wheel. Your eyes are instead drawn to the center, or the hub. Think of the wheel on a BMW, for instance. The emblem of one of the most recognizable car brands in the world is blue and white, and most people say that it reminds them of a white airplane propeller against a blue sky once it begins to spin. The hub is so attractive, we hardly notice the rest of the wheel's parts that connect it with the outer rim and the tire. The hub becomes preeminent, obvious to the onlooker, and this is exactly like your life as a Christian. When life gets going, you want others to see Jesus in you. We all want this! The best way to ensure this happens is to continually build upon the foundations of your faith.

As we turn the corner and wrap up this section of the book, we've looked deeply into four things as our foundations of the Christian faith: developing a love affair with God through His Word and the conversation of prayer, and loving others by cultivating authentic relationships and talking about Jesus. The same foundations apply for everyone who wants to follow Jesus, regardless of age, stage of life, culture, socioeconomic status, or life circumstance, and every time you circle back around with your small batch to study and grow in these practices, God will help you see them in a new light. He'll make His truths come alive for you in fresh, new ways and use the discipleship process as the nudge you need to actually apply them to your day-to-day life. As for the rest of the transformation that occurs along the discipleship journey, God will fill in those holes through your life-on-life time together. It all comes out onto the table as you get to know one another, the struggles you face, scars from the past, the shackles of sin, your hopes and dreams, marriage and children, finances, sex, work, health, etc. Don't try to fix one another. Simply open up your life to them and they to you, seek God together, and love one another through it all. God will take care of the rest.

KEY CONCEPTS

- Worship and fellowship with other believers, as well as inviting those outside the family of God to meet Jesus, help you more fully know and adore God.
- Life-on-life relationship is an important part of discipleship.
- The good news of the gospel is this: God himself came down into His own creation in the form of a man, Jesus Christ. He lived the one and only perfect life, died a sinner's death on a cross as our substitute, was buried, and was raised back to life with victory over death. God offers forgiveness and eternal life to all who believe in Jesus and follow Him.
- Jesus said to "repent and believe in the gospel" in order to be saved.
- You are here on earth today to be God's presence and truth in the lives of all the people He has placed around you.
- The Holy Spirit prepares the "soil" of people's hearts to hear and respond to the Word of God.
- Evangelism methods: *God, Man, Christ, Response*; one-verse evangelism (Rom. 6:23); listening to others' stories with a bridge to the gospel; sharing

your own faith story; asking how you can pray for others (i.e., waiter or waitress).

DISCUSSION QUESTIONS

1. In what areas of your life have you experienced an authentic, life-giving community? What characteristics of that community would you like to extend into your small batch experience?
2. Are you comfortable sharing who you really are with others and the struggles you're going through? What hurts or hangups get in the way of your ability to be vulnerable with others?
3. Have you ever had the privilege of leading someone else to faith in Jesus? Describe that experience. If not, has this ever caused you to feel ashamed, embarrassed or guilty? Read 1 Cor. 6:3-9. How might this truth encourage you?
4. Share a brief version of your faith story, or the testimony of your journey with God, with one another now.
5. Practice sharing the gospel now in your own words using the *God, Man, Christ, Response* method.
6. Who do you know that needs to hear the good news of the gospel of Jesus Christ? How will you share it with them? Take a moment now to pray for these people by name.

part
three
Leading Discipleship

chapter seven

You Are
a leader

If your actions inspire others to dream more, learn more, do more and become more, you are a leader.[1]

John Quincy Adams

Once upon a time, I gave college tours to incoming freshmen. They were the backwards-walking kind, where I tried to avoid face planting while highlighting interesting tidbits of history and folklore around campus. In life, people tend to follow others who are confident and enthusiastic about where they are heading. It's true, don't you think? Great leaders are like this. They blaze trails. They create change. They know the way, lead others with confidence and enthusiasm, and they're not afraid to do things differently than everybody else.

Here's where you come in. There is a fantastic dichotomy involved in your life as a disciple of Jesus: you follow Jesus *and* lead others to Jesus simultaneously. Paul conveyed this idea when he said, "Follow my example as I follow the example of Christ" (1 Cor. 11:1). As long as you've got the order right, the people who follow you as fellow disciples will ultimately be walking in the footsteps of Jesus. But take care! It's all too easy to get that piece wrong and to allow the pride that often accompanies leadership to seep into your heart, pointing others to yourself instead of to Christ.

To be sure, you and I are leaders in the Kingdom of God because of Jesus alone. We have nothing of eternal significance to offer someone else apart from pointing them to Jesus Christ. We've been afforded the unmerited opportunity to influence others spiritually by the invitation and appointment of God. We're leaders in the Kingdom of God, it's true. But also true, we're turtles on fence posts. Let me explain.

YOU ARE A LEADER

Throughout history, God has raised up leaders to accomplish His will. If you scour the whole Bible, you won't find a single person, apart from Jesus, that God chose to lead others who was the perfect candidate for the job. It's the same in the marketplace, really. There's not a leader out there who has stepped into leadership for the first time who felt 100% capable and ready for the job. And yet, they were chosen. Just like those folks, you and I have been chosen to serve others out of love and use our everyday influence for His glory. Matt Chandler says it this way, "God ultimately raises up leaders for one primary reason: His glory. He shows His power in our weakness. He demonstrates His wisdom in our folly. We are all like a turtle on a fence post. If you walk by a fence post and see a turtle on top of it, then you know someone came by and put it there. In the same way, God gives leadership according to His good pleasure."[2]

You are a leader. Being a leader shouldn't be about

making a name for yourself or achieving worldly accolades, and I have to remind myself of this all the time. Similarly, you don't have to have an advanced degree, executive title, or scores of letters behind your name to be a leader. Whatever your story and station in life, you have the opportunity every single day to influence all those around you, and that's leadership. My guess is you're already doing this. Is your interpersonal influence all you'd like it to be, though? If you slow down long enough to evaluate the imprint you want to have on the people around you, especially spiritually speaking, would you choose to live your life somehow differently than you are today? What if you decide right now to do just that, to intentionally invest in others in support of God's purposes in their lives? Is your everyday leadership pointing others to Jesus?

I've been working with leaders for more than two decades in the marketplace, and I've observed some who struggle and others who thrive. I think there are important life lessons that can be learned from this latter group. Gifted leaders have a way of inspiring you. It's easy to spot them. They are bold in their dreams and passionate about making a difference in the world. Great leaders build others up in order to help them reach their greatest personal potential and cheer them along on their journey. Great leaders multiply their impact in this world because, when it comes to teamwork, one plus one is greater than two. And of course, the leaders who have the greatest impact are ultimately those who set out to serve. It was never about them in the first place. Selfless living unleashes the potential of others because it's born out of a foundation of love.

For even the Son of Man came not to be served but to serve others and to give his life as a ransom for many.

Mark 10:45

Greater love has no one than this: to lay down one's life for one's friends.

John 15:13

So, let's imagine that as a disciple and disciple-maker, you've been chosen to lead (which you have), just like a new manager in the workplace. How do you get off your turtle shell and get started? Simon Sinek, in his powerful and popular TED Talk and subsequent book, *Start With Why*, offers that human motivation starts with the "why," meaning that before you and I are willing to jump into anything, we have to first understand our purpose.[3]

It's worth a pause here to be sure you understand the purpose or "why" behind discipleship. If it's still a little fuzzy, you may want to go back and reread Part I of this book. But as a quick recap, our greatest purpose as Christians is to enjoy a loving relationship with God and to help others do the same. We're disciples of Jesus who make other disciples of Jesus as we are going along our way in life, whether it's to work, the grocery store, the soccer field, inside our homes, out for tea or coffee, or on vacation. It's the way Jesus did life, it's the command He gave us, and to top that off, He promises He'll be with us every step of the way when we do it.

We get to be part of what God is doing in the world, we allow others to add to our own spiritual journey, and we fall more in love with Him in the wake of His grace. This is our purpose, and it's bigger than anything we could have drummed up on our own. This is our spiritual anchor — using our whole selves and our whole lives to positively impact and lead others to God.

Leadership is influence - nothing more, nothing less.[4]

John Maxwell

Think for a moment about the people in your life who have had the greatest influence on you. Take a quick pause and entertain me by doing a brief reflective exercise. Get out a piece of paper and pen, or scribble in the margin of this book. With one minute on the clock, write down the names of 3-5 people who have had the greatest positive impact on your life. Now, before you keep reading, if those people are still alive and you have the ability to contact them, take the time to write them a quick note to tell them how much they've meant to you and how they impacted your life in such a special way. Next, take a look at your list. I wonder who those influential people are whose names you jotted down? As many times as I've done this exercise with leadership audiences, I'm guessing that some of the people on your list include the following: a teacher, coach, parent, mentor, or friend. For me, some of those heroes have been: my high school biology teacher, Mr. U, who inspired me; my cheerleading coach, Coach Melanie, who told me she believed I'd go far in life; my first boss, Rob, who took a chance on me; my professional mentor, Cheryl, who shared her time and brilliance to help me dream about my future; Herb, the man who discipled my husband and I and who God used to change our whole perspective on life. My heartfelt thanks are owed to each of them, as well as my hubby, parents, and three amazing kiddos, whose influence in my life I'll never get over.

When we think of "influencers" in society today, we usually think of famous people who have a large social media following, presence on the big screen, loads of money, or political power. But those people didn't end up on your list, did they? And, why not? What is the distinguishing factor between those who reach "influencer" status and those who really have a life-changing impact on the trajectory of your life? Time and again leaders have told me that having a personal relationship is the difference-maker. Those people on your list have (or once had) a personal relationship with you; therefore, real influence is a matter of relationship. If you want to influence others or to make a positive difference in other people's lives, you have to earn that right by building a relationship with them. You have to care about them and care *for* them, intentionally carving out time with them to build trust. Once trust is established, they'll open the door for you to speak into their lives. This is a key step in a new leader's journey, and it's an equally important factor in a successful discipleship relationship.

The first job of leadership is to love people.[5]

Rick Warren

Anyone privileged to disciple another Christ-follower sits in a sacred seat of accountability and dependency on the Lord. It's a big deal to potentially be one of the few who end up on someone else's "influencer" list. And over the course of time spent together, you will most likely touch on one or all of those roles I listed earlier as the discipler: teacher, coach, mentor, parent, and friend.

TEACHER

Let's start with the first one: teacher. It's clearly laid out in the command Jesus gave us that we will be teaching others. In the Great Commission, Jesus said to make disciples by "teaching them to obey all that I've commanded you." So, after helping others to more fully identify with Christ, you'll explore together what God's commands are and hold one another accountable to living them out.

How do you feel when you hear this idea that you're called to be a teacher? Oftentimes I hear from other people that they really don't feel like a natural teacher and, therefore, they think the teaching thing should be left to someone else. That's obviously not what Jesus said, though, and experience shows that the teaching process is just as beneficial for the discipler as it is for those they are teaching. Research backs this up. A 2018 study cited in *Applied Cognitive Psychology* confirmed that the act of teaching itself improves the teacher's learning because it compels the teacher to cognitively retrieve what they've previously studied.[6] In other words, teaching actually strengthens the neural pathways that allow you to remember things you've learned and makes it easier to apply them to your everyday life. Teaching is, thus, an effective learning method. As the Latin proverb suggests, "By learning you will teach, by teaching you will learn." Our understanding and our obedience will increase as we are accountable and prayerful to teach others. I think Jesus knew this to be true as He called us into the lifelong learning journey of discipleship.

How do you teach? Keep it simple. Make the most of the time you have together, and consider using your group time more for discovery and application of biblical truths and concepts, than simply for intake of information.

- Create a space where learning and growth can occur. Use this book.
- Dig up or create other activities, illustrations, or stories that bring the gospel to life.
- Share what you're learning in God's Word with your disciples, and ask them to share what they're learning with you.

- Ask challenging and thought-provoking questions of your small batch.
- Read spiritually challenging books together. Readers are leaders!
- Use videos and podcasts that spur you along, and talk with each other about how to apply the concepts to everyday life.

MEET ANGIE

Angie teaches elementary school in an inner city school district. As a teacher, she's constantly learning new teaching techniques to stay on top of her art. One of those techniques is the "gradual release method." The idea is: I do, we do, you do. What if we discipled this way? Might that create real behavior change in our lives?

As a teacher, Angie also knows she doesn't have to have all the answers, rather she does everything possible to help her students find them. You can be a learning catalyst, too! Ask your disciples spiritually thought-provoking questions, and let them ask questions. Deep ones. Don't be afraid when you don't have all the answers, just go find out together. Then, give them the challenge of re-teaching important lessons back to the group, or even to a friend or a neighbor, kind of like a student teacher might do. When they're ready to launch out and try this whole thing for themselves, help your small batch world-changers organize their notes and materials into an orderly and re-teachable curriculum that can be easily repeated with their own disciples, who can repeat it with theirs.

COACH

Disciplers are coaches, as well. A great coach is likely

under the wings of any successful athlete, and the same is true for high performing spiritual teams. Coaches set a high standard and inspire players to hone their skills with excellence. They watch for progress and put players in the game when they're ready, huddling afterwards to debrief and celebrate the team's victories. Coaches build a strong team and create a culture of trust, fun, and mutual commitment.

In his book, *The Coaching Habit*, Michael Bungay Stanier encourages leaders in the workplace to tame their inner Advice Monster, stopping themselves from interrupting and slipping into fix-it mode while coaching others, especially when trying to help them develop.[7] Stanier adds that coaching for development goes beyond simply solving the problem someone's facing and instead focuses on the *person* who's trying to solve the problem. Rather than continually dispensing advice as a disciple-maker, give yourself permission to instead listen and point your fellow disciples to the Word of God to find solutions. It's like the old adage that teaching someone to fish is better than simply giving them the fish. Make it a habit each week, then, to ask your disciples what they've learned since you last met. If you're leading more than one person at a time, ask your group to weigh in when someone presents a question or issue before answering it yourself. Before you know it, you'll be coaching your team toward mutual discovery and transformative learning.

MENTOR

Disciplers are spiritual mentors. Similar to coaching, mentorship is another hot practice in the marketplace right now. High potential professionals often have multiple mentors throughout their career, who help them move successfully from one phase of life to the next. What do the most effective mentors do? For starters, they look for mentees who are motivated by and committed to personal growth. Mentors ask meaningful questions that help steer the mentee toward the goals they've set for themselves. They share lessons learned from their own experiences and are open to learning new things alongside their mentees. Look for disciples, therefore, who are serious about their own journey with Jesus and are all-in on the small batch experience. Then, invite your disciples to identify several spiritual goals they have for themselves, and thoughtfully craft experiences and discussions throughout your journey together to help them achieve those goals.

In today's business landscape, it's also true that sometimes "reverse mentorships" occur, where a younger mentor brings fresh perspective and energy to a more seasoned mentee. There's probably something to be said for that, too, in the discipleship arena, yet another example of how discipleship can be a two-way street.

Be a connector. Mentors connect people. They don't see themselves as a sole source of information, but rather they help make connections that enable their disciples to benefit from others' expertise, as well. Mentors use an outside perspective to help their mentees make sense of the puzzle pieces of their life. Finally, mentors give their mentees permission to dream big dreams, suggest stretch assignments to help prepare them for future success, and paint the expectation from the very beginning that they should, in turn, pay forward the investment made in them into others' lives in the future.

Over the past year, I have benefited so much from participating in a professional mentorship journey of my own, where I reflected upon all that God has been doing in my life, at work, at home, and in ministry. My mentor listened to me, cheered me on, held me accountable to my own goals, asked great questions, learned with me, connected me with others who could help me, and affirmed the gifts and passions that she saw in me. She helped me make sense of the big-picture portfolio of my life, including my life experiences, on-the-job skills, personal passions and aspirations, and to imagine how I might merge all of this together to love and serve others with unique purpose. Her time and wisdom made a huge impact in my life. Mentorship like this can be another significant connection point between discipler and disciple, as a small batch leader can serve others in this very same way.

PARENT

Next, let's not forget the toughest and most important job on earth: parent. Jon and I prayed and tried for quite some time before we were able to have our first child. Waiting was really hard, and we were prepared to embrace any picture of parenting God had in mind for us, but thankfully we were blessed with the opportunity to raise three amazing kids. As any parent can attest, raising children is kind of like running an uphill marathon in a sea of sprinkles, equally hard and wonderful. Meanwhile, relying on God to help me continually display the life of Christ to our kids as we embrace the roller coaster of life together has shaped this momma to be more like Jesus through an overwhelming string of humbling moments.

According to God, raising children includes a responsibility to love and raise your kiddos in the ways of the Lord. What a stunning privilege and responsibility! As parents who've also committed to making disciples, Jon and I have become increasingly convinced in our home that a key tenet of parenting our children in the ways of the Lord is for them to routinely see us giving of ourselves and investing in others' lives generously. While the tug on a parent's heart to sacrifice any measure of family time is real, ultimately the refreshment you receive inside your small batch as a weary parent helps you return to your family bearing greater fullness of life. This is a very helpful thing! Meanwhile, discipling during the parenting seasons of life also involves inviting others into your messy moments. Remember, your disciples benefit from learning what it looks and feels like to be a normal, imperfect family who seeks after the Lord *and* chooses to pursue a Great Commission lifestyle. This sets them up to do the same within their own families one day. Finally, as they watch you make disciples in your home, your children will be inspired by those individuals, who will, of course, seem way cooler than you. Your kids will be proud to know they're an important part of Team Jesus, sharing their parent(s) with others and adopting an others-oriented worldview, which they will hopefully themselves embrace for a lifetime. Keep these things in mind as you consider sitting out any season of life from making disciples, or encourage someone else to do so. And regardless of one's life stage or family size, it's also true every discipler is a spiritual parent for those they lead to Christ and for the members of their small batch, an equally unimaginable privilege and responsibility!

What do great parents do? *What do they not do?* Parents feed their children and nurture their growth. They teach their kids practical skills that will serve as the foundation for life on their own. They love their children, even when they don't fully understand or appreciate the sacrifices made on their behalf. Parents encourage their children to follow their example where it's most critical, but also to put their own spin on things as they grow and mature. Wise parents adapt their parenting approach to suit the unique needs, preferences, and personality of each child. They create a safe environment in the home where every member of the family feels valued, loved, and accepted. Finally, they set boundaries where they are helpful. As a spiritual parent, these are all true of a discipler.

Throughout the New Testament, Paul refers to Timothy, Titus, and Onesimus as his *true sons*, and to the believers in the churches he planted as his beloved *children*. While obviously not Paul's biological children, it's fair to say they were his spiritual children because he shared the gospel with them and raised them up in the faith. It's because of Paul's spiritual parenting and God's work through him that each was born again into the spiritual kingdom and became children of God. Paul loved his spiritual kids and grandkids deeply, and he continued to nurture their spiritual and social health even after departing by writing letters, returning to visit, or by sending a friend to care for them in his absence.

A loving parent never gives up on their kids, and one day, when they're ready, they get to launch their children out into the world, encouraging them to chase after their wildest dreams. If the two of them maintain a strong relationship into the next phase of life, most find their relationship reaches a whole new level of fun and friendship. Also true in the small batch!

FRIEND

A sweet friendship brings joy to the heart (see Prov. 27:9). So lastly, disciple-makers are good friends to those they lead in faith. As friends, disciplers listen to their disciples and spend time simply doing life together. They slow down enough to be fully present. They rejoice when their disciples are happy and hurt with them when they're sad. Friends make life more fun and meaningful, and so does the small batch.

I recently had the privilege of launching out my eighth group of disciples, after wrapping up a nine-month discipleship journey together. This time around, the discipleship journey overlapped with one of the most turbulent times in my life. Although it wasn't easy while enduring personal trials to continue to set aside regular time for teaching them and nurturing our relationship, I found the sacrifice more than worth it. While I continued to serve them, those friends of mine strengthened and encouraged me as their discipler in ways I couldn't have possibly imagined beforehand. I couldn't have foreseen what was over the horizon, but because God sovereignly crafted us together for precisely this time, they never wavered in commitment to me once the storms set in. I'm as grateful for my small batch sisters as they ever could be for me. Now, equipped with a solid foundation of spiritual community and biblically-based knowledge and practice, they have launched out to embrace their greater purpose by paying forward this investment into other women's lives. And as for us, we'll be friends to the end.

Many people will walk in and out of your life, but only true friends will leave footprints in your heart.[8]

Eleanor Roosevelt

EXAMPLES IN THE BIBLE

The Bible provides us a personal example of all five of these relationships within a discipleship context.

Luke used research and writing as the primary tools to **teach** his disciple. He left no stone unturned in gathering first hand information to impart unto Theophilus, the recipient of Luke's gospel writings and, at first, a gentleman still considering the claims of Christ. As a medical doctor and all-around smart guy, Dr. Luke continually added to his own storehouse of knowledge and pursued answers to life's biggest questions on behalf of others. Luke took it upon himself to personally interview subject matter experts and witnesses who knew Jesus in order to ensure the information he entrusted to Theo was an accurate portrayal of Jesus Christ. He systematically arranged his teaching materials to provide an orderly account of the gospel (Luke 1:1-4) and continued building him up as their relationship matured (Acts). We would expect nothing less from a physician researcher!

In one of Dr. Luke's treatises to Theophilus (Luke 10:1-24), we are invited to sit in the grandstands and witness for ourselves coaching at its finest as he retells a story about Jesus with his disciples. Jesus, rightfully an example of all five of these roles, might be a surprising candidate for **coach**. As Luke explains, though, Jesus trained a team of 72 to be champions for the gospel by rehearsing the plays together of performing miracles and spreading the good news. Then, he checked them into the "game" two-by-two and put their skills to the test. The disciples returned to huddle up with Jesus afterward, and together they debriefed. Coach Jesus and his team celebrated their victories and thanked the Father for Kingdom wins.

You might be wondering about an example of a biblical **mentor** in the Bible. Well, look no further than Moses. Moses went down in history as the only prophet of Israel with whom God met face-to-face and who uniquely demonstrated God's miraculous power before the people (Deut. 34:10-12). But all along the way, he'd also been preparing his successor and mentoring him to step in once he was gone and lead God's people into the Promised Land. Moses began by offering Joshua a stretch assignment, building up his leadership skills as commander of his army. Moses stood on the hillside during the battle, holding high the banner of the Lord with a balcony-level view of the entire experience. Afterward, at God's command, Moses recorded the events to help Joshua see God's hand in it all and always remember how the Lord had led him to victory (Exod. 17:14-16). Joshua accompanied Moses everywhere as his right-hand man, and Moses brought his protégé right to the feet of the Lord (Exod. 24:12-14), shared authority with him in front of others, and positioned him for future leadership (Num. 27:18-23, Deut. 34:9). Over the course of their time together, Moses made sure his mentee was ready to courageously step into the special leadership role God had for him. As a mentor, Moses always had one eye on the next generation.

While on the subject of generational discipleship, we now turn to the heartwarming story of Ruth and Naomi. Young Ruth's reputation of loyal love and kindness toward her mother-in-law and **spiritual parent**, Naomi, preceded her (Ruth 2:11-12). Ruth had grown in a decade's time to have such trust and affection for this woman, she never hesitated in following Naomi back into the land of Yahweh once their husbands had both died, despite knowing she would likely face considerable hardship as a foreigner among God's people. You see, because Naomi had loved her so dearly (Ruth 1:8-14) and taught her the ways of the Lord, Ruth was able to say with conviction, "Where you go I will go, and where you stay I will stay. Your people will be my people and your God my God" (Ruth 1:16). As the course of events unfolded in their lives, the pair moved as one from hopelessness and desperation to obedient faith and overflowing joy. And as always true between spiritual parents and offspring, their relationship was mutually beneficial, for Ruth blessed Naomi's life far more than she ever could have asked or imagined (Ruth 4:13-22, Matt. 1:5).

Finally, while Jesus calls us his **friend**, He also graces us with the gift of friendship with our fellow disciples. Together in small batch style, Mary and Elizabeth were there for one another as the unexpected twists and turns of life unfolded. God's plans for both of their lives were unanticipated to say the least, one pregnant after a lifetime of infertility and the other expecting a baby long before the required events for that to take place had occurred (Luke 1:5-38). What would people think? What would they say? Nevertheless, the two encouraged one another's faith in God's promises and raised a hallelujah right there in Elizabeth's living room (Luke 1:39-56). They reminded each other that nothing was impossible with God (Luke 1:37). Maybe you need a friend like that. I do.

When God aligns your heart and mind toward this noble purpose of spiritually investing into another human being, He will undoubtedly enable you to play all the roles you need to *when* you need to. Don't worry if you don't get it all right every time, because none of us will. Keep in mind that God deeply loves you just as you are, sees you as His masterpiece (Eph. 2:10), and rejoices over you with singing (Zeph 3:17), so there is no striving needed to knock this out of the park. God will accomplish it in and through you. Therefore, embrace the influence God has given you. Look for the best in people and call it out. Invest in the next generation, and cheer them along. Serve others with love in small, everyday ways. Little things, when multiplied, add up to a spectacular whole.

Remember, life is not a zero-sum game, where one person's loss is another person's gain. There is room for *all of us* to simultaneously do our very best in life and fulfill our God-given potential. As a matter of fact, I'm convinced there is a need for all of us to do this. So let me encourage you now to pursue the world for Christ in just the way God designed you to. Write that book you've been dreaming about writing. Sing the song that echoes in your heart. Paint your painting. Pitch the big idea. And while you're at it, gather a new small batch to seek Jesus together, and encourage them to go boldly, too. The world desperately needs us all, as the body of Christ, to work together as one team and inspire this same spirit in those we lead.

If you want to go fast, go alone. If you want to go far, go together.

African proverb

LEADERSHIP CASE STUDY

Sometimes it's helpful to consider a real-life scenario after the fact to glean lessons that apply to our lives today. John F. Kennedy said, "Leadership and learning are indispensable to each other."[9] In that spirit, let's dive into a short case study and examine the leadership characteristics of Paul toward those he led to Christ in Thessalonica. Paul was excellent at making disciples of others while still following Jesus himself, and his example should prompt you to consider your own practices as a spiritual influencer for Jesus. Let's journey for a moment into the land of Thessalonica and take a peek at the relational landscape between Paul and his faith family.

The books of 1 and 2 Thessalonians were penned by the Apostle Paul around 50 years after Jesus came to earth. Having just endured brutal physical abuse and imprisonment in the city of Philippi, Paul and his companions were called to go and share the gospel in the region of Macedonia. Accordingly, Paul traveled there right away, along with his young disciple, Timothy, and Silas, a peer and partner in ministry. Once in Macedonia, they strategically entered the bustling Roman port town of Thessalonica, which served as the economic and cultural center of the region. A melting pot of numerous cultures, religions, and travelers from around the world, competition was heavy for the attention, and perhaps even the money, of anyone who might stop to listen to fellow journeymen with a message to share.

Paul went straight to the synagogue, and he joined those who gathered regularly there to discuss, debate, and reason together about the scriptures. The Bible records that Paul explained and persuaded them that Jesus was the long-awaited Messiah, and that he suffered, died, and rose back to life in order to earn eternal life for all who would follow Him. Some Jewish listeners (i.e., religious people), many non-Jewish Greeks (i.e., non-religious people), and a large number of prominent, wealthy women believed the gospel message and began to follow Paul as he followed Christ (1 Cor. 11:1). A church was born.

The passages in these two books are really personal letters Paul wrote to encourage the new Thessalonian believers in their faith, given that he himself was chased out of town just three weeks after arriving. As you might imagine, those with positions of power within the Jewish church and local society quickly became jealous and resented the loss of influence brought about by this new King Jesus, about whom Paul preached. *Does this sound like office politics to anyone else?* Once the dirty work of chasing Paul out of town was finished, they turned their thuggish focus to dissuading his converts from the Christian faith. Would their faith be strong enough to stand up to trial and temptation? Would they return to the ease and privilege they once enjoyed before choosing to follow Jesus? Paul was concerned about this, and he longed to continue encouraging them in their faith journey, even if only by letter.

How had Paul accomplished so much here in just three weeks' time, winning the lost and setting up a self-sustaining community of faith that would live on after he was gone? And how enduring really was his influence for the Lord in Thessalonica? Paul's legacy for Christ did indeed stand the test of time, and God continued to mature and leverage his Christ-like leadership characteristics for the sake of the Kingdom.

The final test of a leader is that he leaves behind him in other men, the conviction and the will to carry on. [10]

Walter Lippman

There are those leaders who rise into new positions of influence with humility, wisdom, and relational prowess, but just as many struggle to transition from measuring success by their own performance to instead defining success by how well they are able to help others achieve their goals. This is frankly the greatest transition any leader has to make: letting go of being an expert or superstar themselves, to instead helping and highlighting others. This mindset adjustment is key, shifting one's mental model from self-focused to others-oriented. We who follow Christ have been commanded to do just that (Matt. 28:18-20), to grow and develop others as we ourselves continue to spiritually mature. Success for Paul wasn't about making a name for himself, but rather using his influence to help others succeed and grow in their relationship with Christ. He focused every moment he had in Thessalonica toward building up the new believers to stand firm in their faith once he was gone. His labors indeed bore fruit.

You did not choose me, but I chose you and appointed you so that you might go and bear fruit - fruit that will last - and so that whatever you ask in my name the Father will give you.

John 15:16

Back to the Book. Paul started his letter in 1 Thessalonians by signing his name. Letters of his day were written on rolled-up scrolls of papyrus paper that had to be unrolled to be read, so identifying the author had to be done at the start. He then boldly declared Jesus and the Father as one, graciously greeting both Jews and Greeks in verse two with a message of grace (*charis* in Greek) and peace (*shalom* in Hebrew). Everyone was included in God's invitation, as Jesus made a way for all to come to God the Father! Paul went on to praise the Thessalonians and tell them how proud and grateful he and his team were for their strong, joyous faith. Their lives had changed so dramatically, as Paul described, that people were already talking about them throughout Macedonia and everywhere their feet and boats journeyed. A changed life is powerful evidence for the grace and goodness of God.

Let's not miss the leadership lessons we see already. Paul was inclusive in his recruiting of new Christ-followers, indiscriminately sowing the seeds of the gospel much like the farmer in the parable of the soils (Matt. 13:1-23). Armed with truth and his own life story, Paul boldly shared the message of Christ and his vision for others to join him in the mission of God because he knew it was in their best interest to do so. He longed to see everyone receive the opportunity of salvation that he'd been afforded, and many did join him. Paul connected the dots for new believers, helping them see how their lives were already being used for the sake of the gospel all around the world, as people were talking near and far about the changes they'd seen in them. He warmly affirmed them by writing, "Therefore encourage one another and build each other up, just as in fact you are doing," (1 Thess. 5:11). Their small batch community of faith would endure and multiply only to the extent they continued to do this.

We loved you so much that we were delighted to share with you not only the gospel of God, but our lives as well.

1 Thessalonians 2:8

Paul continued on with this letter, defending the pure, others-oriented motives of his ministry. How else could he have endured such suffering and still charge boldly into Thessalonica to share Christ? The compassion he had for them, which stemmed from the love God first showed Paul, is what continually propelled him forward. Paul and his team loved the new believers so much that they were delighted, overjoyed even, to share with them not only the truth of the gospel but their own lives, as well. As the old saying goes, "Others don't care how much you know until they know how much you care." Paul cared for them by sharing the good news of the gospel courageously, calling them to repent and believe in Jesus Christ. He discipled them in their newfound faith by teaching them to understand the scriptures, modeling ethical, holy behavior, and practicing with them the skills of the faith they would need to continue after he was gone. Paul allowed them, with a spirit of vulnerability, to examine his own struggles and failures as much as his strengths and victories. Finally, Paul continued to teach, challenge, and encourage them after he was forced to flee town, via letter, and by sending his friends to visit them.

This is exactly the type of leader people want to follow, a humble leader who makes much of Christ and not much of himself or herself. This applies to you, too. The people around you are keenly aware of their own imperfections. How else will they envision themselves being used by God, apart from seeing God use you despite, maybe even because of, *your* imperfections? Do you want to lead others as you follow Christ? Then, follow Paul's lead and be all about others. Open your life up to others with humility and compassion. Begin to define your own success by helping others develop and grow. Squashing down pride and self-centered ambition, press into another believer's life from whom you can learn, gather the best discipleship toolbox you can, and invite others along to pursue Christ together. The lives you touch with the hope of Jesus Christ will be multiplied one-by-one until eternity begins, and there may be no greater leadership opportunity than this. You will truly live, according to Paul's words (1 Thess. 2:19, 3:8), when others stand firm in the faith because of God's work in and through you.

MEET ASHLEY

Ashley prayed for nearly eighteen months for all the pieces of the puzzle to fall into place to embark upon her first disciple-making mission trip to South Africa. When the time finally came, she and her team joined those who gathered from nearby farms, villages, and churches at a retreat center to seek Jesus, the view from their huts decorated with nearby giraffes. Over the course of a weekend's time, they explored Paul's investment into the Thessalonian church and their response to the Gospel as new believers, including many of the truths you just read about in this chapter. Meanwhile, Ashley and the team laid their lives, and their comfort zones, down for the sake of the Body of Christ. They pressed pause on their everyday pursuits and held all that is most dear to them with open hands in order to travel across the globe, obediently trusting that God would use this sacrifice in a mighty way. They ate steaming hot food with their bare hands, and layered on bath towels as clothing for extra warmth during the early morning hours, as the locals did. They learned to pray out loud the way so much of the rest of the world's believers do, with boldness, and to dance while they worshipped God like no one was watching. Serving humbly behind the scenes, as well, the team prepared food for hundreds. You see, Ashley and friends had prepared for this trip for months prior, and when the time came, they did everything possible to help this moment touch eternity for all who gathered in His Name. One tiny small batch team of Jesus-loving women used their own life stories, and even their professional giftings such as personal fitness in Ashley's case, to encourage and challenge all those who would soon depart back into surrounding African towns and villages.

Within this act of surrender, God's hand was all over things. As a matter of fact, at one point, Ashley was seated outside, teaching a lesson on spiritual fruit. Without even noticing it, her group had circled up their chairs right under an orange tree. Ashley held up an orange in one hand, which she'd grabbed earlier from the kitchen, to illustrate the fruit God grows in our lives as believers. Instantly, another orange fell from the tree above into the lap of her translator; because, of course, the translator was saying and doing the exact same things as Ashley but didn't have a piece of fruit to hold up. They all held their breath for several seconds in order to process what just happened. Amazed, all they could do was laugh in worship. It's the little things that happen all around us that keep us looking up, don't you think? God's fingerprints were all over the details of this moment, just like they are on our lives today.

The conference ended with a bang. Leaders from each church represented at the event celebrated with gifts, a slideshow of pictures, and a beautiful recap of all the teaching. In a moment of culmination, one of the pastors stood and issued a challenge to the entire group. Having heard the riches of God's Word delivered at this event by teams traveling from afar for ten years by this point, she urged the crowd that they not allow one more year go by without each making one personal disciple of their own. She humbly asked God to start with her. Over the next year, they committed to share all they'd learned at the retreat with someone else and to invite others to join them on their journey with Jesus. This is the harvest! Some planted, others watered (1 Corinthians 3:6-9). Ashley was one of the lucky ones to see the sheaves brought in. After years of groundwork, God's people got it. They really got it.

Great leaders work themselves out of a job. They're all about raising up that next generation. They labor hard and invest deeply, and then they cheer, as those whom they once lifted up now go on without them. Others-oriented leadership is what disciple-making is all about. The lifestyle of discipleship modeled by Paul, and of course first by Jesus Himself, is where true love, joy, and hope abound.

For now we truly live since you are standing firm in the Lord.

1 Thessalonians 3:8

I have come that they may have life, and have it to the full.

John 10:10

KEY CONCEPTS

- Leaders cast a meaningful vision and engage others to bring it to life. They invest in the next generation and cheer them along. They serve from a foundation of love.
- You are a leader because of the influence you have on all those around you, and influence is a matter of relationship.
- Disciple-makers often serve in the roles of: teacher, coach, mentor, spiritual parent, and friend.
- Paul led many men and women to Christ in Thessalonica and quickly began to disciple them in their newfound Christian faith. Paul and his small batch ministry partners loved the new believers so much that they were delighted to share with them not only the gospel of God, but their own lives as well.
- The measure of great leadership is others' success.
- Your greatest leadership opportunity is impacting other people's lives with the hope of Jesus Christ and building them up through discipleship to stand firm in the faith.

DISCUSSION QUESTIONS

1. Can you relate with the "turtle on a fence post" idea? Explain.
2. Describe your relationship with one of the people on your personal influencer list. Why did that person have such a special influence in your life?
3. Which role of the discipler mentioned in this chapter do you most identify with: teacher, coach, mentor, spiritual parent or friend? Why?
4. What do you think must have transpired between Paul and the new Thessalonian believers in order for them to grow from new Christian converts into a healthy, self-sustaining church within just three weeks time? What lessons can you take from this?
5. The new believers in Thessalonica faced tremendous hardship upon professing faith in Jesus Christ and chose to give up societal privileges they once knew. What worldly things, experiences, or relationships do you struggle to hold before the Lord with open hands?
6. Paul says, "For now we truly live since you are standing firm in the Lord," (1 Thessalonians 3:8). What do you think he meant by "truly living"? How might this connect with Jesus' statement in John 10:10?

chapter eight

Vision &
multiplication

Leadership is building a bridge that connects the vision with the purpose, in order to empower those who are around us. [1]

David Walker

GOD-SIZED VISION

Great leaders are visionaries. I often remind the leaders I work with how important it is to frequently make connections for their teams between the big-picture mission and the everyday work they do. This is important because when people get in the grind of their daily tasks, whatever they are, it's easy to lose sight of how one person's small contribution fits into the bigger whole. Paul did this with the Thessalonians, as we saw in our case study. The truth is, leaders in any organization have a balcony view; they see and hear things about the mission and vision of their organization that others aren't exposed to nearly as often. It's the leader's responsibility, then, to personally communicate those messages in an effective and impactful way, enabling each member of the team to sense they're part of something bigger than themselves and that they're making a meaningful difference in the world. After all, it's a core desire of all human beings to do so. Forbes Human Resources Council suggests while nearly two thirds of employees in the marketplace are disengaged in their work, those who *are* engaged feel this way largely because their company mission is clear and their contribution as a part of the team is recognized.[2] Similarly, according to research by Harvard Business Review, people find more meaning in their work when they can see how it impacts those they serve.[3] When a connection like this is made between our life's work and the bigger picture, a deep sense of value and engagement follows.

Spiritually speaking, the Bible allows every Christ-follower to see and hear the saving truth of the gospel, and we understand through our interactions with the people around us how each of our lives fit into the bigger picture of the Kingdom of God. We've been given the balcony view, and it's a privilege, an unimaginable grace. It's our responsibility, therefore, to share that which we've seen and heard with others. The "team" of humanity is desperately searching for ways to feel both valued and valuable, to find their purpose and to leave a mark on this world. As Christians, we must steep ourselves in God's Word in order to see things from His perspective, and then to share our God-sized vision with those around us.

What is vision? According to the dictionary definition, vision is sight, the anticipation of something yet to be, the experience of a divine appearance, imaginative conception, or a scene or person of extraordinary beauty.[4] Read that definition again. Doesn't this description perfectly characterize

Jesus? God in the flesh, Jesus is both divine and beautiful. In order to get a clear view of who the Lord really is, though, we need God to grant us spiritual understanding. We need to ask that He illuminate His Word for us and bring it to life inside our hearts and minds. Jeremiah 33:3 says, "Call to Me and I will answer you. I will show you great and unsearchable things that you do not already know." Sadly, if we as His people don't ever truly see the big picture of who Jesus is and how our lives are meant to personally multiply the life of Christ, our potential impact on this earth will be greatly reduced and the effects will be tragic.

Where there is no vision, people perish.

Proverbs 29:18 (KJV)

What does the word "perish" in this passage mean? The Hebrew word used here is *para*. (Go ahead and look it up in your *Blue Letter Bible* app.) It means losing restraint, going to pieces, being exposed or naked, rejecting good counsel, and dying. Therefore, where vision is lacking in our world today, society goes unbridled and people careen toward their own destruction. Today's headlines certainly don't disagree. The world today knows what it means to perish.

In 2020, what once seemed possible only in a sci-fi novel or Hollywood movie became a strange and unexpected reality. Again, the entire world experienced the impact of a global health pandemic, as millions of people contracted COVID-19 coronavirus, likely many more without reported symptoms. Hundreds of thousands died, and no populated area of the globe was immune. Suffering extended beyond the virus itself though. In addition to staggering illness and mortality, the world also experienced financial strain, unemployment, breakdown to the food supply chain, social isolation, and emotional distress. In the U.S., a federal emergency hotline for people in emotional distress reported a 1000% increase in calls in April 2020 over the same time period a year prior.[5] Schools and churches were forced to close their doors, weddings and graduations were missed, and patients passed away in hospitals without their loved ones permitted to be in attendance.

Still, the human spirit was very much alive with hope. Even while stay-at-home orders were in place, voices rang out to all who would hear that we were "alone together." New Yorkers clapped from their windows at the hour of shift change to cheer on local healthcare heroes at the hospitals, and Coloradans howled into the mountain air to signify a resilient pack mentality.[6] Birthday parties became drive-by parades, musicians played from their front porches, and friends met in parking lots to enjoy happy hour from the backs of their cars. In small moments, families took walks, enjoyed more meals at home, prayed, and spent time together in the absence of the hectic schedule they'd become accustomed to. Crisis revealed one major truth: We need one another. When we are kept apart, we hurt.

Shalom, the Hebrew word for "peace" found throughout the Bible, is the greeting God's people have used with one another for centuries. It's got quite a ring to it. The meaning goes much deeper than a 1960's flower-power peace; rather, it means harmony with God and with one another, a put-back-togetherness where once torn apart. Peace is the opposite of perishing. According to Proverbs 29:18, to avoid perishing, we have to start with vision.

I've heard it said before: you will become what you behold. Said another way, you will be like what you look at. On any one given day, what are you looking at? What images, advertisements, books, shows, or role models fill the gallery of your mind? Second Corinthians 4:18 says to fix your eyes on what is unseen. The Kingdom of God must be front-and-center on the dashboard of your life. You need to see the world as Jesus sees it and to get on your heart that which is on God's heart. So the obvious next question is: what *is* on God's heart?

Dawson Trotman, founder of The Navigators organization, equated spiritual vision with getting on our hearts what is on God's heart - the world.[7] Nailed it! *People* are what's on God's heart, a whole world of perishing people who desperately need to find themselves in the arms of the One True God who recklessly adores them. Meanwhile, the vast majority of the world's people are, at best, poorly evangelized, with nearly half of the billions living today never even having heard the name of Jesus Christ. If we as Christians really believe what we say we believe and take Jesus at His Word that He is the Way, the Truth and the Life, and that no one comes to the Father except through Him (John 14:6), then this cannot be okay. By default, if Jesus is exclusively all of these things, then everything else people put their hope in is a lie. Therefore, the most loving thing we can do for other people is to do everything possible to make Jesus Christ known.

For I am not ashamed of the gospel, because it is the power of God that brings salvation to everyone who believes: first to the Jew, then to the Gentile.

Romans 1:16

In 2012, I had the opportunity to participate in a disciple-making mission trip to Honduras. Our team was led by my brother and sister in the faith, Soup and Linda Campbell, whom Jon and I both treasure as co-ministers of the gospel and look up to as mentors in the faith. I brought with me two fellow disciples, one a seasoned traveler and another who had never left the country, the latter of which inquired about where she'd plug in her curling iron and blow dryer during our time on the mission field. As we arrived at the departing airport, Soup welcomed the team and proceeded to share we'd be kicking off our journey in what had recently been named the most dangerous city in the world. That's one way to start your gathering! As the week unfolded, we slept on mattresses on the floor covered in tiny bugs. The females and white guys on the team hid in the back of our vehicles to minimize the risk of kidnapping or endangering the team. We entered prisons while praying we'd make it back out again. We hiked up slippery, mud-covered mountain sides to reach remote places with the good news of the gospel. It occurred to me I'd have some explaining to do with my untraveled friend's doting husband when we returned. That last scene, though, was the one that shook me to the core.

After a day's hike in the mud, uphill both ways of course, we arrived at a tiny rain-soaked home. It was dark by this time, and we were starving. The host family offered their precious resources in the form of something hot from a boiling kettle upon our arrival, and we ate, food sanitation rules tossed aside. The team gathered inside a humble shelter, wooden benches lining the room and a tin roof ringing over-head with the sounds of the rainstorm. The night was young.

People from nearby settlements began to arrive, some having walked for hours in the downpour along dark, slick, rocky mountain trails. The benches began to fill up. More came. It was standing room only. Some members of our team stood up to address the crowd and shared their faith stories of how they met Jesus and the ways He had made a difference in their lives. People kept coming. A simple sheet was draped up front and a projector was powered up. We'd brought with us a copy of the "JESUS" film, and while it played, so many people piled inside the room that my team and I stepped back out into the rain to create additional space.[8] Maybe you've heard the term "darkening the doorway of a church" before? Locals were literally squashing in against one another under-neath the door frame just to catch a glimpse of Jesus...in the dark, in the rain. All of this simply to *see* Jesus! I was undone.

Here's what they knew: just one glimpse of Jesus brings life. How's that for spiritual vision?

What about the earliest leaders of the church? How did they share the vision and mission of Jesus? In the book of Acts and beyond, early followers boldly proclaimed the gospel both near and far. Would they have been satisfied to sit on the bench, as we so often do today, when the opportunity and need around us is so great? No way! The early church was laser focused on equipping normal, everyday church members, the saints, to love God and engage in the work of the ministry by sharing Christ and making disciples of others (Eph. 4:12). They carried the gospel to new places and preached the Word boldly. But let's not forget, before there were pulpits and projection screens, there were tables and chairs. Early Christians *gathered* in kitchens and living rooms. They *invited* friends, family, and those in their social circles. They served, loved, and healed with hospitality. They *saw* one another and, together, looked to Jesus.

The mission was *others always*. The early church devel-oped individuals and invested into faith families who immedi-ately and continually pursued their own calling to do the very same. Today, rather than focusing on building outward-oriented individuals who count for the Kingdom, we typically focus instead on creating bigger and better institutions and events. This is inward growth, perpetuating and protecting the environment where we can comfortably hear a preacher do the work of the ministry with a warm beverage in hand. To be sure, I love warm beverages being in hand, but when the battleship training ground of the Church becomes the cruise ship experience for the masses, I fear we've lost sight of Jesus' mission and vision altogether. When the work we unleash the saints to do is limited to tending the parking lots, nurseries, and welcome centers of our institutions, we cripple the body and shortchange the intent of Heaven.

Francis Chan, in his book *Multiply*, says this, "God's

church is not a social club. It's not a building, and it's not an option. The church is life and death. The church is God's strategy for reaching the world. What we do inside the church matters."[9] Church leaders of today, we need to pivot. We need to equip, empower, and unleash the massive potential sitting on the pews and in the auditoriums of our churches for the sake of all those they know, meet, and have the potential to meet. Discipleship is not a neat and tidy church program or offering; rather, it is every member of the Body on mission in their own unique thirty-foot sphere of influence. And if done right, very quickly the influence of Jesus moves out of the building and gets unmanageable from the pulpit, out of control even, in all the right ways. It's not a paint-by-number masterpiece in the making, it's Picasso.

THE ART OF SPIRITUAL LEADERSHIP

There is an art to great leadership. Every leader builds upon the foundations of solid leadership practices, such as those we've discussed, by putting their own signature touch on how they lead. They incorporate their own personality, passions, and talents into the work of serving others. This is true of us as Christ-followers, too. Jesus clearly commanded us to make disciples. He didn't, however, leave instructions for one and only one way to do this. Perhaps, thus, there is an art to discipleship, as well, and a uniqueness to each small batch. Meanwhile, knowing how serious Jesus is about this calling, the command which he used his last breaths on earth to convey, we'd better think seriously about the best way to personally fulfill the mission He has for our lives. French novelist and activist, Émile Zola, once said, "The artist is nothing without the gift, but the gift is nothing without the work."[10] If your heart's desire is to truly follow Jesus, an examination of Jesus' own method of making disciples must be followed by actually *doing* the work, applying what you've learned to small batch relationships of your own and putting your signature touch on the discipleship process.

In case it would be helpful to bring this vision back into focus once more, think back on what Jesus did with His earliest disciples while physically on Earth. How did Jesus do it? The short answer is He invited regular, flawed people in need of a Savior to join Him (Matt. 4:19), and the only requirement was that they follow. Jesus brought them up close long enough to teach, show, and equip them, then He sent them out (Mark 3:14). Known at first as disciples, meaning lifelong learners and followers of Jesus Christ, at one point in the Bible Jesus' followers were henceforth presented as "apostles" (Luke 6:13, Eph. 4:11). The Greek roots of this word found throughout the New Testament are *apo*, meaning away from, and *stolos*, or sent. Therefore, after spending a period of time with Jesus, His disciples became the very ones sent out with the message of the gospel. As a matter of fact, Jesus used a form of this same word, *apostelló*, when He told them after the resurrection, "As the Father has sent me, so I am sending you" (John 20:21).[11]

It was a global mission and vision for every follower of Jesus Christ, and so it is today. If you are His, then you are both qualified and called to do this work. God will use every unique thing about you as fuel for the journey: your passions, pains, life experiences, knowledge, and skills. Make no mistake, Jesus fully expects every one of His followers to have a vision and a strategy they're willing to give their entire lives to in order to continually impact the world for the Kingdom of God, from our neighborhoods to the nations. The great news is God didn't leave us wondering what that vision and strategy should be. Not only did God show us the way, Jesus literally became the Way.

WE HAVE A VISION PROBLEM

What if we don't? If you and I choose not to use our lives to pursue the vision and strategy of Jesus via discipleship, then there will be less put-back-togetherness in the world and fewer people seeing Jesus for who He is. Sadly, most folks inside the church today are clueless about the fact that this Great Commission command to make disciples of others applies to our own lives individually, and not just to professional ministers. If we're honest, most feel even more clueless about *how* to go about doing it, even if they really want to. We have a vision problem.

Most Christians haven't actually seen a Great Commission lifestyle modeled before them in a way that helps to appreciate what's expected. Taking that one step further, once they see it, they need to be skillfully enabled to replicate that lifestyle themselves. Calling all leaders! (That's *you*!) The church at large has lost sight of the fact that the benches must be cleared and sent out onto the field ready to play. The playbook is in hand. We need to start scrimmaging within our holy huddles and get reps to every member of the team, rather than eating hot dogs and drinking cokes in the grandstands, watching the pros alone taking the field. Sports analogies aside, everyday people like you and me must begin to walk out a discipleship lifestyle in our homes, schools, and workplaces, one small batch at a time. Eventually, if we do, the influence of Jesus will be multiplied beyond our wildest imaginations. We need a vision that is so big, so God-sized, if it actually happened it could only be explained by an act of God. We need to look no further than the life of Jesus to see how this is done.

STRATEGY OF MULTIPLICATION

It's overwhelming to imagine how one small, ordinary person like you or me could seriously make an impact on the world that would touch the very ends of the earth. How could this be? After all, you've got enough on your plate just worrying about yourself that even the idea of embracing a God-sized vision and mission might make your brain throb. Take one final pause, and let's look again at scripture to see how God explains this.

After Jesus voiced His discipleship-focused parting words, He returned to Heaven physically and left mankind the gift of His Holy Spirit (John 14:16). The Holy Spirit, like Jesus minus flesh and bones, moved in and began walking around on this earth through individual believers as the "Body" of Christ. Beginning on the Day of Pentecost, a new way of experiencing God's presence was used to empower and propel the church out like a rocket. I picture this first handful of apostles like dice coming out of a Yahtzee cup, flying out in every direction. As a result, God's presence can be found today in every nook and cranny where Christ-followers live and go.

On this historic day of Pentecost, our friend, the beloved Apostle Peter laid out for the crowd before him the life, death, and resurrection of Jesus, and the coming Holy Spirit, in sermon form. Three thousand people were added to the number of early believers that day (Acts 2:41). Let that sink in. Do you remember who this same Peter once was? He was *not* a polished speaker and leader, to be sure. However, God used Peter in precisely that way, speaking out on His behalf and leading others to Christ. God is never limited by our weaknesses.

God continued adding more and more members to the church every day (Acts 2:47, 5:14), until so many people were added to their number they couldn't keep count anymore. It was out of control! Just then, a significant change happened worth noting. God's strategy for growing the early church changed from addition to multiplication (Acts 6:1 - *plethyno*, to multiply), accelerating and never again reducing back down to addition.[12] Jesus' strategy today remains the same: *multiply* your life in Christ by making disciples of others.

Paul invested spiritually into a young guy named Timothy, and they became so close to one another over time that he called him, "Timothy, my son" (1 Tim. 1:2, 2 Tim. 1:2). He discipled him. Paul encouraged Timothy to hold onto all he'd heard from him as the pattern of sound teaching (1 Tim. 6:20, 2 Tim. 1:13-14). Timothy was then to entrust those very same things into the lives of other faithful people, who would then be qualified to also teach them to an untold number of generations of Christ-followers to come (2 Tim. 2:2). Four generations of Jesus-followers are pictured in this verse: Paul, Timothy, Timothy's disciples, and many to follow. This is how one-and-one become two, two multiply into four, and four eventually reach the ends of the earth.

Just for fun, especially if you're keen on mathematics, try to figure out how many times it would take you to double one individual person into two, and then four, and so on, until you had more than the entire population of people on earth today. You'd be shocked to learn how few times it would take for this doubling exercise to outnumber humanity. For example, in 2020 the earth's population was close to 7.8 billion people.[13] How long would it take using multiplication for one person to reach the entire world for Christ? The answer is less than half the average lifetime! If one disciple of Jesus spent a year investing into the life of another individual, which is entirely reasonable, and then both of them repeated the process with someone else the next year, and those four people did the same thing the following year, then eight, then sixteen, and so on, the entire world's population could be effectively discipled as followers of Jesus Christ in fewer than 34 years. Shocking, right? Get out some scratch paper or your trusty calculator and test me on this. Now, what if God chose to align *more* than just two people at a time in our small batch relationships? Can you even imagine the potential? God's math is no joke. Jesus wanted us to follow His example to reach the world because it's really the only way to accomplish it.

Did you ever play the game of telephone as a kid? You remember. It's where you sit in a circle with a group of people, one person thinks of something to say, they whisper it to the person sitting next to them, who passes it to the next person, and on down the line. When the message gets to the last person in the circle, they announce loudly to the group what they heard. Everyone laughs, of course, because the final message is never anywhere close to the original. This is exactly what we do *not* want to happen in discipleship.

The disciples you make will, in all likelihood, teach and do with their disciples exactly what you've done with them. Take caution here. If you fail to challenge them to live a life of holiness, then how much more will they fail to seek holiness with their own disciples. If you omit one or more of the foundations of the faith in learning or practice, your disciples will be ill-equipped to lead others in that space, too. For example, if you are reluctant to share the gospel and skip over the evangelism component, rather than allowing the discipleship process to stretch you out of your comfort zone through accountability to your small batch, you'll impair the body of Christ and many may never have the opportunity to hear about Jesus. The same goes for studying scripture, prayer, and for fellowship with other believers. If you are faithful, however, and give everything possible to that next available woman, it's very likely you won't be able to keep up with the names and faces of those whom your disciples will one day impact, and that's exactly how it should be.

Since leaders have the balcony view, as we discussed earlier, then what they're overlooking could be considered a dance floor. You and I are the chosen leaders in this movement of Jesus. He has entrusted the mission to us. When you jump in, you join the great dance of the Kingdom. Imagine an illustration of disciple-making acted out using dance moves. A few people go outside the room while one person teaches another person a series of dance moves. The series is hard to remember and takes some practice to get the moves just right. The two dancers talk and practice together until the second person is confident enough to bring someone else in from outside the room and reteach them the dance. The process continues down the line, until the last person from outside repeats the dance moves exactly like the first. Of course, the style and abilities of each dancer plays a role, but the pattern is the same and the end result is multiplication of the dance.

Every time I've seen this illustration played out in real life, even cross-culturally, there are moments when each dancer has to step outside their comfort zone and feels a bit awkward as they're learning. The key to success, though, is that every dancer has the chance to keep working one-one-one with their teacher until they're ready to bust a move. Can you see the parallels? We're all learning a great dance as we go along in life, sometimes following and other times taking the lead. But if we continually invite others in, we can practice the moves together, stretch the limits of what we once thought we could do, and share the dance floor with those to come. Cue the music!

Remember, spiritual leaders help others find their place in the big story God is still writing in our world today. Leaders invite others to be on their team and build them up to reach their greatest potential. Leaders help others see Jesus for who He is and learn to walk with Him. Because the difference they make is multiplied, a leader's impact on this world is so much greater than if they simply did life on their own. You are a leader! And you can do this.

THE LAST SIP

It's your turn now. You are officially called to lead others to Jesus while following after Him together. Continue to make disciples by:

- Exploring discipleship together;
- Practicing the fundamentals of the Christian faith, and;
- Building your disciples into leaders who can go and do likewise.

This is the pattern to repeat from here on out. Let it settle into the deep places of your heart and transform the way you live each day going forward. It's through making disciples the small batch quickly becomes something much, much bigger.

And as you are going, be faithful in the small things. Live there. Breathe deeply there. Our lives are filled with them: small batch circles of faith, small moments and conversations, small opportunities and duties, small glimmers of hope, sparks of creativity, tiny whispers of an idea, little ways to show a lot of love. Yes, be faithful in the small things, for in the end we'll discover they were the only ones we ever truly held in our hands. And when we join hands with one another, we'll find God handcrafts us all together into something beautiful and grand.

KEY CONCEPTS

- Spiritual vision is having on your heart that which is on God's heart.
- The vast majority of the world's people today are, at best, poorly evangelized, with nearly half of the billions living today never having heard the name of Jesus Christ.
- The early church focused intensely on equipping normal, everyday people to love God and do the

work of the ministry, which is sharing Christ and making disciples of others.

- If you are a Christ-follower, then you are both qualified and called to make disciples. The difference you make in this world for the Kingdom of God is greater when you make disciples, because your impact is multiplied.
- If every Jesus-follower today discipled one other person per year, and they each repeated the process every subsequent year, the church could impact all of humanity with the gospel of Jesus Christ in less than thirty-four years.
- A Great Commission lifestyle involves:
  o Falling in love with God.
  o Seeking out the wisdom and encouragement of more mature believers.
  o Praying for and inviting others to join you as you follow Christ.
  o Putting a plan in place to study and practice the fundamentals of the Christian faith with your disciples.
  o Allowing God to make you more Christ-like as you grow.
  o Sending out your disciples to make other disciples when they are ready.
  o Repeating this process until Jesus returns or calls you home.

DISCUSSION QUESTIONS

1. Reflecting upon this statement, "You will become what you behold," how does what you look at or watch influence who you are today and who you

are becoming? (Hint: Consider books, websites, t.v. shows, people, scripture, etc.)

2. Do you ever struggle to see how your everyday tasks fit into the big picture of God's Kingdom work? What encouragement can you take from this book as you ponder the special role God has for you to play?

3. How does Jesus' earthly example of making disciples, as well as your own unique personality, life experiences, passions, and talents, inform how you see yourself living out a Great Commission lifestyle in the future?

4. Search through the book of Acts to find all instances of addition and multiplication. What does this tell you about God's strategy for the growth of His Church?

5. Read Revelation 2:4. Discipleship starts with loving God. Thinking back on the time when you first loved Jesus, has your love for the Lord grown colder or warmer over time? If colder, how might you stir your affection for God today?

6. Have you ever sought out the wisdom of a more mature believer as a source of challenge and encouragement in your life? If so, describe that person and your experience with them. Who can serve you in this way today?

7. Who has God placed on your heart to invite to join you in your adventures with Jesus? What fears do you have about talking to them about discipleship? Pause now and pray for God's help in this area.

conclusion

Small Batch Discipleship is meant to kick start your discipleship journey and serve as foundational content you return to again and again. So, what do you do now that you've finished reading this book? My ask is that you do *anything* other than set this book down and move on to another new thing.

Remember, as a disciple, first you are to personally seek the Lord and fall head-over-heels in love with Him. There's nothing worth multiplying if you aren't rooted in a loving relationship with Jesus, and you're not ready to lead others spiritually unless you're first being led by God. It's my prayer you've grown in your love affair with the Lord while you've journeyed with me through this book. So seek Jesus right now, and keep seeking Him always.

Don't stop there, though. It's time to multiply! You're ready to make disciples of your own now, so I encourage you to find at least one or two other people and invite them to join you in re-reading the book. In the corresponding *Small Batch Discipleship Leader's Guide*, you'll find a sample layout for a customizable six to twelve month discipleship journey, with experiential activities to take your adventure up a notch. God may grant you more or less time than six months with each person you disciple, and that's perfectly acceptable. Make this work for you, and trust God to fill in any gaps according to His sovereign grace.

Don't forget: your village affects your vision. Over time it will be increasingly important to stay in close contact with other believers who are also committed to making disciples and running with Jesus. Keep rubbing shoulders with other disciple-makers. Keep inviting others along. Rinse and repeat.

One final story. For years, Jon discipled men in a high

security state prison, something I was very proud to support in prayer and through sharing our time with him while our kids were very small. After several years of serving there, one of Jon's disciples was released and began rebuilding his life in the free world. The impact of Jon's belief in him and the investments he'd made into his life were so significant that he asked Jon and our oldest son to be in his wedding. What an honor! After the ceremony, which was absolutely precious and unlike any I'd seen before, we crossed over the tracks to the other side of town for the reception. When we arrived after dropping our son off with a babysitter, the party was already in full swing. The food line was nearly tapped and every seat was taken. Jon opened the door. Like a scene in a movie, the party stopped, and everyone turned and looked at us. We searched the room for the groom, whose gaze warmly met ours. Immediately he got up, walked over to meet us, put his arm around our shoulders, and personally escorted us to the head table. The bridegroom had actually saved *us* a seat!

We eventually made our way onto the dance floor that night and got our wobble on, but the illustration of our entrance wasn't lost on me. It didn't matter the colors of our skin, our backgrounds, or our current life situations, we were one family. We belonged together because of the chain-break-ing, boundary-defying love of Jesus. On our own, we don't belong in Heaven, but because of the love of Jesus, He has saved us a seat at the head table. We are His people, and He has invited us into the party.

What are you waiting for? The Bridegroom is looking for you. Once you make your way into His embrace, once you're in the door and part of the Great Dance, it'll be up to you to keep dancing until Jesus returns or calls you home. Remember, it's never too late to come inside. It's never too late to start pouring your life out for the sake of someone else. In every season and until the glorious end, let's live this life well, friends. Here's to the small batch!

acknowledgements

How do you even begin to thank the people who have helped you along the way? I honestly still don't know. Everything in this book, and everything in me, is a result of the love, wisdom and presence of others. My heart is full.

Thanks to all those who made this book what it is today. To Judy West for giving me both your gut check personal reactions to this book and your eagle eye. It's smarter and more relevant because of you. To Kadi Cole for validating that this work is important and encouraging me to press forward when my next steps were as clear as mud. To Lindsey Hartz at Hartz Agency, for your creative genius and for putting a plan in place that got this book into readers' hands. I love watching you honor your faith story by the way you serve others. And to the team at MRM for your hard work behind the scenes on the edits, layout, and cover design for this book.

To all the leaders over the years who have invited me into their professional journey, taken my words seriously, chosen to be courageously vulnerable, and taught me what it means to lead well, my humble appreciation.

Thanks to Greg Ulmer for being the coolest teacher ever and filling your classroom with life and inspiration. How could anyone top learning biology with a bird on your shoulder? Thanks to Melanie Bishop for believing in me as a person and making sure I knew it. You bring new meaning to the word "cheerleader." To Rob Sanders for taking a chance on me as a young professional. I've multiplied the investments you made in me far and wide. And to Cheryl Throgmorton, who showed me how mentors learn from and alongside their mentees. You are a beautiful example of humility, curiosity and lifelong learning.

Thank you to my *Small Batch* sisters in Christ. You've taught me more than I've taught you, and you give my life greater meaning. Thank you for linking arms with me. Please know I'll never stop approaching the throne of grace on your behalf, and on behalf of every disciple and life you touch. I'd be remiss without a few special shout-outs. Jenn de Berge, I'm inspired by how you've made discipleship your most passionate vocation. Thanks for being my friend during my most wayward days, and for encouraging me to daringly pursue my gifts in ministry today. I'm not sure I would've had the audacity to do it without your nudges. Morgan Harrington, your artwork is a vessel of God's grace, and all those around you are drawn like a magnet to Jesus in you. May every disciple of Jesus who reads this book be blessed by your beautiful "abide" artwork in the leader's guide and find rest for their souls as they put color to page. Emily Lindsey and Lauren Geyer, thank you for speed reading, even enduring tornadoes together, as you helped get this book ready for others, and dreaming with me about all the ways to bring this big idea to life.

To Greg Holder for inviting us into *echad* and reigniting a spirit of creativity in me as a teacher. My most heartfelt thanks for lighting a candle in the darkness. Your gifts make it safe for those still considering the claims of Jesus to draw near to the cross, and for those of us who follow Him to swim more deeply in the ocean of grace together.

Warmest appreciation to Soup and Linda Campbell for trekking arm-in-arm with Jon and I into prison and all over this globe. Thank you for being real with us. You inspire us to keep things spicy and to go boldly together forever for Christ. I'll always watch for the doors to swing open on the mission field in the hopes you'll be there. Stay cool.

To Herb and Judy Hodges, there aren't enough words. Your imprint on our lives is all over these pages. We love you.

To Cheri Holcomb, for helping me cultivate a heart for

discipling other women. May God keep bringing you tulips.

To Ken and Ashley Anthony, thank you for the Jesus car, and for fanning the flame of Christ with us from day one.

And to Ron Surgeon. You share the gospel with the coolest words anyone has ever heard, and I'm pretty sure Jon and I both want to be you when we grow up. Thanks for all the late nights seeking God's fame around our kitchen table. One God for the globe.

To Ashley and Michael O'Hare, long live team O'Sully. It's been rare for us to get to enjoy intimate discipleship with both a husband and wife together, and the time that we've gotten to spend with you has always been an easy "heck yeah." Thanks for flying in busted up airplanes and catching oranges that fell from the sky with us. Let's do it again.

To Barrett Jones, for bear-hugging our kids, giving them a diehard Jesus-loving guy to look up to, and running our grocery bill up for a year - seriously one of our favorite years yet. There will always be a place at our table for you and Katie.

To Case & Kimberly Keenum, you've inspired so many by sharing your story, the ups *and* the downs, and you encouraged me to share mine. Keep on living out the discipleship lifestyle like you have been, from the locker rooms to your living room. As fellow members of Team Jesus, we'll be forever cheering you both on from the sidelines.

Deeper still...

To Jon, my bike-riding, estate-saling, music-loving partner in life. This life is a roller coaster of adventures, discoveries, struggles and dreams. We've had our share of all of those, and I'm grateful to have been by your side for every one of them. Thank you for encouraging all my wild ideas and not laughing me out of the room every time I spun up another one. Thank you for loving me and for introducing me to Jesus. May His glory be all over every word of our story forever.

> *Don't urge me to leave you or to turn back from you. Where you go I will go, and where you stay I will stay. Your people will be my people and your God my God.*

Ruth 1:16

To Tyler, you make me feel special every day, and there is nothing that could make me more proud than you telling me you can't wait to hold my book in your hands. I hope you feel Jesus on every page. Thank you for inspiring me every day by caring for me and others so deeply, and by giving everything you do all you've got. You can truly do anything you set your mind to. May your identity be wrapped up in who God says you are, and may you always feel as loved and encouraged as you make others feel just by being you.

> *Therefore encourage one another and build one another up, just as you are doing.*

1 Thessalonians 5:11 (ESV)

To Callie, whose creativity, tender concern for others, and fiery spirit make you a mighty force. You are my little ladybug, and I've dreamed about making disciples of others together with you from the first day I knew you were within me. Here's to horses and chickens and all the things that stir your affections for our Creator God. May the sparkle in your eye never dull, and may you keep singing and dancing for joy all your days.

Satisfy us in the morning with your unfailing love, that we may sing for joy and be glad all our days.

Psalm 90:14

To Matthew, my eyes well up at just the thought of you. I have been praying over you since the first days in your nursery and haven't stopped since. You are brave, bright and strong. Little ones adore you. You have a unique curiosity and gifting that will enable you to figure out how anything in this world works. Most importantly, you stand to bring a message of hope to those who need it most. May your life be a bright light shining into the darkness for the gospel's sake.

For God has not given us a spirit of fear, but of power and of love and of a sound mind.

2 Timothy 1:7 (New King James Version)

To my mom, you are my hero. You bring joy to every occasion, and your laundry smells like a breeze from heaven. You also never give up, and you're generous beyond measure. You've been my greatest cheerleader and the one constant in my life, and I thank God for you every single day. I'll never get over how you love me! May the ways I live my life and love others bring honor to the way you've lived yours.

I thank my God every time I remember you.

Philippians 1:3

To Dan, thank you for accepting me as your own and covering me with boundless love and affection. You've carried couches and boxes all over this great country for your girls, danced with us on your toes, hugged, consoled, called, and sent flowers at all the right times. You've inspired each of us to keep casting our lines out in life.

To my sisters, I admire and love you both dearly. You're amazing mothers, loyal friends, and wicked smart boss ladies. Our family will always be the best one on earth. Let's keep laughing and lingering forever!

To my extended family, you've been the writing between the lines of my life story.

And finally, to my Lord Jesus Christ, thank you for pursuing me to the ends of the earth and calling me your own. You've wrapped me up with your love, helped me to see you and to know you, and surrounded me with some of the most amazing people on the face of the planet. You have given my life greater purpose than I could've ever dreamed up on my own, and you continually satisfy this adventurer's soul. I know I'll never deserve one dash of your relentless affection, but I will use every breath you give me to sing your praises, shout your glory, and whisper my gratitude until you bring me home. Help me to always trust you, no matter what, and may my story point others to you in all things.

May the God of hope fill you with all joy and peace as you trust in him, so that you may overflow with hope by the power of the Holy Spirit.

Romans 15:13

recommended
resources

Additional Resources on Discipleship:

- *Small Batch Discipleship Leader's Guide (Available for download at tracysullivan.com)*
- *Knowing the Bible 101: A Guide to God's Word in Plain Language (Christianity 101®)* by Bruce Bickel and Stan Jantz
- *Master Plan of Evangelism* by Robert Coleman
- *The Cost of Discipleship* by Dietrich Bonhoeffer
- *With Christ in the School of Prayer* by Andrew Murray
- *Pray for the World: A New Prayer Resource from Operation World* by Jason Mandryk, Molly Wall
- *My Utmost for His Highest* devotional by Oswald Chambers
- FaithLife Study Bible app
- Blue Letter Bible app
- *How to Have a Daily Quiet Time* guide by The Navigators*
- *One-Verse Evangelism: How to Share Christ's Love Conversationally & Visually* by The Navigators*
- *My Heart Christ's Home* booklet by Robert Boyd Munger*

* free pdf available online

Additional Resources on Leadership and Relationship:

- *Emotional Intelligence 2.0* by Travis Bradberry and Jean Greaves

- *The Five Love Languages* by Gary Chapman
- *Love & Respect* by Emerson Eggerich; see also *Love & Respect in Parenting*
- *The Art of Gathering: How We Meet and Why It Matters* by Priya Parker
- *Boundaries* by Henry Cloud and John Townsend
- *The Complete 101 Collection: What Every Leader Needs to Know* by John C. Maxwell

about the author

Tracy Sullivan, a seasoned leadership strategist and executive coach, has spent more than twenty years training Fortune 500 leaders and shaping organizational culture in the finance, healthcare, and nonprofit industries. She also speaks and teaches at ministry events and conferences around the world.

Tracy has personally led small batch discipleship groups for over a decade. She lives with her husband, three children, and canine sidekick in St. Louis, Missouri, and is a connoisseur of all things small batch.

You can learn more about Tracy and her ministry at her website: https://www.tracysullivan.com.

facebook.com/tracysullivandiscipleship

instagram.com/tracysullivandiscipleship

pinterest.com/tracysully123

sources

Introduction:

- [1]Vincent van Gogh, "Letter to Theo van Gogh from The Hague," n.d.
- [2]*Bonhoeffer's Cost of Discipleship* (Nashville, TN: B&H Publishing Group, 1999), 21.

My Story:

- [1]Robert Brault, "Quotable Quotes," *Reader's Digest*, September 1986, 139.
- [2]Timothy Keller and Kathy Keller, *The Meaning of Marriage: Facing the Complexities of Commitment with the Wisdom of God* (New York: Penguin Books, 2016), 48.

Chapter One:

- [1]Joan Podrazik, "WATCH: Oprah's Favorite Martin Luther King, Jr. Quote," HuffPost (HuffPost, January 21, 2013), https://www.huffpost.com/entry/oprahs-favorite-mlk-quote_n_2496816.
- [2]*The Proposal* (Touchstone, 2009).
- [3]Lauren Barlow, *Inspired by Tozer 59 Artists, Writers and Leaders Share the Insight and Passion They've Gained by A.W. Tozer* (Grand Rapids, MI: Baker Publishing Group, 2011), 185.

- [4]Rudyard Kipling, *Animal Stories* (Leeds, UK: House of Stratus Limited, 2008), 134.
- [5]Donald Cantrell, *31 Sensational Sermon Snapshots Volume 12* (Morrisville, NC: LULU.COM, 2014), 33
- [6]"G3100 - Mathēteuō - Strong's Greek Lexicon (KJV)," Blue Letter Bible, accessed May 23, 2020, https://www.blueletterbible.org/lang/lexicon/lexicon.cfm?Strongs=G3100.
- [7]Mark Dever, *Discipling: How to Help Others Follow Jesus* (Wheaton, IL: Crossway, 2016), 13.
- [8]Joshua Project, "Joshua Project," Joshua Project, accessed May 21, 2020, http://www.joshuaproject.net/.
- [9]Dallmann, William. Jesus; His Words and His Works According to the Four Gospels: With Explanations, Illustration, Applications, Twenty Art Plates in Colors. United States: Northwestern publishing house, 1914. pg.172
- [10]David Platt and Francis Chan, *Follow Me: a Call to Die, a Call to Live* (Carol Stream, IL: Tyndale House Publishers, 2013), 120.

Chapter Two:

- [1]Morgan Edward Forester, *Howards End* (London, UK: Putnam's, 1911), 227. "Howards End," Google Books (Google), accessed May 23, 2020, https://www.google.com/books/edition/Howards_End/9sBaAAAAMAAJ?hl=en.
- [2]Benecke, Joanna. 100 Reasons to Love Audrey Hepburn. United Kingdom: Plexus Publishing Limited, 2016. (Reason #52)
- [3]Priya Parker, *The Art of Gathering: How We Meet and*

Why It Matters (New York: Riverhead Books, 2020), 42.

- [4]Priya Parker, *The Art of Gathering: How We Meet and Why It Matters* (New York: Riverhead Books, 2020), 236.

- [5]Travis Bradberry and Jean Greaves, *Emotional Intelligence 2.0* (San Diego, CA: TalentSmart, 2009).

- [6]Helen Riess, "The Seven Keys of E.M.P.A.T.H.Y.," in *Empathy Effect: Seven Neuroscience-Based Keys for Transforming the Way We Live, Love, Work, and Connect Across Differences* (Sounds True, Incorporated, 2018).

- [7]"'I Must Have Flowers, Always, and Always.",," VMFA, June 5, 2015, https://www.vmfa.museum/connect/i-must-have-flowers-always-and-always/.

- [8]William C. Compton and Edward Hoffman, *Positive Psychology: the Science of Happiness and Flourishing* (Thousand Oaks, CA: SAGE Publications, Inc., 2019), 380.

- [9]Roach, John, *2,000-Year-Old Seed Sprouts, Sapling Is Thriving* (National Geographic, 2005) Accessed May 23, 2020. https://www.nationalgeographic.com/news/2005/11/051122-old-plant-seed-food/

- [10]Shen-Miller, J., Mary Beth Mudgett, J. William Schopf, Steven Clarke, and Rainer Berger. "Exceptional Seed Longevity and Robust Growth: Ancient Sacred Lotus from China." *American Journal of Botany* 82, no. 11 (1995): 1367-380. Accessed May 23, 2020. www.jstor.org/stable/2445863.

Chapter Three:

- [1]"God Wants More for You Than You Do," Desiring God, accessed May 23, 2020, https://

www.desiringgod.org/articles/god-wants-more-for-you-than-you-do.

- [2]Nicholas Genes, "Ben Franklin and the Bifocal |," Medgadget, May 8, 2018, https://www.medgadget.com/2005/07/ben_franklin_an.html.
- [3]"G1689 - Emblepō - Strong's Greek Lexicon (KJV)," Blue Letter Bible, accessed May 23, 2020, https://www.blueletterbible.org/lang/lexicon/lexicon.cfm?Strongs=G1689.
- [4]Quotes of Michelangelo, accessed May 23, 2020, https://www.michelangelo.org/michelangelo-quotes.jsp.
- [5]"Harriet Tubman," Biography.com (A&E Networks Television, January 16, 2020), https://www.biography.com/activist/harriet-tubman.
- [6]Debra Michals, "Harriet Tubman," National Women's History Museum, accessed May 23, 2020, https://www.womenshistory.org/education-resources/biographies/harriet-tubman.
- [7]Person, "Harriet Tubman," Christian History | Learn the History of Christianity & the Church (Christian History, February 21, 2016), https://www.christianitytoday.com/history/people/activists/harriet-tubman.html.
- [8]C. S. Lewis, *The Weight of Glory and Other Addresses* (New York: HarperOne, 2001), 26.
- [9]T. S. Eliot, Christopher Ricks, and Jim McCue, *The Poems of T.S. Eliot* (London: Faber & Faber, 2015), 938.
- [10]TruthBeTold Ministry, "Easton's Bible Dictionary & World English Bible: Matthew George Easton: NOOK Book," Barnes & Noble (TruthBeTold Ministry, January 16, 2018), LII. https://www.barnesandnoble.com/w/eastons-

bible-dictionary-world-english-bible-truthbetold-ministry/1127859931.

- [11]Malcolm J. Gill, *Knowing Who You Are: Eight Surprising Images of Christian Identity* (Eugene, OR: Wipf & Stock Publishers, 2015), 22.

Chapter Four:

- [1]Austin O'Malley, *Keystones of Thought*, (New York: Devin-Adair Company, 1914), 138. "Keystones of Thought," Google Books (Google), accessed May 23, 2020, https://www.google.com/books/edition/Keystones_of_Thought/IbsXAAAAYAAJ?hl=en.
- [2]Andrew Murray, *Absolute Surrender* (Nashville: B & H Publishing Group, 2017), 149.
- [3]"Abide," Merriam-Webster (Merriam-Webster), accessed May 23, 2020, https://www.merriam-webster.com/dictionary/abide.
- [4]"G3306 - Menō - Strong's Greek Lexicon (KJV)," Blue Letter Bible, accessed May 23, 2020, https://www.blueletterbible.org/lang/lexicon/lexicon.cfm?Strongs=G3306.
- [5]Lecrae (@lecrae). 2013, "Success Isn't What You've Done Compared to Others. Success Is What You've Done Compared to What You Were Made to Do." Twitter, May 29, 2013, 10:19 a.m., https://twitter.com/lecrae/status/339747921740300288.
- [6]Taysha Murtaugh, "15 Famous Love Letters That Every Die-Hard Romantic Needs to Read," Country Living (Country Living, January 24, 2018), https://www.countryliving.com/life/inspirational-stories/g4061/famous-love-letters/.
- [7]"Deconstructing the Kingdom of Self,"

PaulTripp.com, accessed May 23, 2020, https://
www.paultripp.com/wednesdays-word/posts/
deconstructing-the-kingdom-of-self.

- [8]Robert Browning, *Rabbi Ben Ezra* (United States:
Thomas B. Mosher, 1909), 5. "Rabbi Ben Ezra,"
Google Books (Google), accessed May 23, 2020,
https://www.google.com/books/edition/
Rabbi_Ben_Ezra/1cxEAAAAYAAJ?hl=en.

Chapter Five:

- [1]"Bear Bryant," Biography.com (A&E Networks
Television, April 13, 2019), https://www.
biography.com/athlete/bear-bryant.
- [2]"Throwback: Paul 'Bear' Bryant Talks about
Philosophy: Coach & Athletic Director," Coach
and Athletic Director, January 31, 2020, https://
coachad.com/articles/coach-a-d-throwback-paul-
bear-bryant-talks-about-philosophy/.
- [3]Bill Thrasher, *A Journey to Victorious Praying: Finding
Discipline and Delight in Your Prayer Life* (Chicago:
Moody Publishers, 2003), 77.
- [4]David John Lu, *Overcoming Barriers to Evangelization
in Japan* (Eugene, OR: Wipf & Stock, 2019), 115.
- [5]Kay Arthur, *Lord, Teach Me to Pray in 28 Days*
(Eugene, Or.: Harvest House Publishers, 2008), 6.
"Lord, Teach Me to Pray in 28 Days," Google
Books (Google), accessed May 23, 2020, https://
www.google.com/books/edition/
Lord_Teach_Me_to_Pray_in_28_Days/
Pe2EAQAAQBAJ?hl=en.
- [6]"Silent and Solo: How Americans Pray," Barna
Group, accessed May 23, 2020, https://www.
barna.com/research/silent-solo-americans-pray/.

Chapter Six:

- [1]Piper, John. Desiring God: Meditations of a Christian Hedonist. United States: Multnomah, 2011. pg.141
- [2]"U.S. Adults Have Few Friends-and They're Mostly Alike," Barna Group, accessed May 23, 2020, https://www.barna.com/research/friends-loneliness/.
- [3]"New Research on the State of Discipleship," Barna Group, accessed May 23, 2020, https://www.barna.com/research/new-research-on-the-state-of-discipleship/.
- [4]Jonathan Holmes et al., "Biblical Friendship Cannot Be Hacked," The Gospel Coalition, July 28, 2016, https://www.thegospelcoalition.org/article/biblical-friendship-cannot-be-hacked/.
- [5]Lewis, C.S.. Joyful Christian. United Kingdom: Scribner, 1996. pg.192
- [6]Brené Brown, *Daring Greatly: How the Courage to Be Vulnerable Transforms the Way We Live, Love, Parent, and Lead* (United Kingdom: Penguin Books Limited, 2013), 37. "Daring Greatly," Google Books (Google), accessed May 23, 2020, https://www.google.com/books/edition/Daring_Greatly/3rF7vvXa_yIC?hl=en.
- [7]C. S. Lewis and Kathleen Norris, *Mere Christianity: a Revised and Amplified Editions, with a New Introduction, of Three Books Broadcast Talks, Christian Behaviour and Beyond Personality* (San Francisco: HarperCollins Publishers. Harpers San Francisco, 2001), 71-72.
- [8]Herb Hodges, *Tally Ho the Fox: the Foundation for Building World-Visionary, World-Impacting, Reproducing Disciples* (Memphis, TN: Spiritual Life Ministries, 2001), 194.

- [9]"Apollo 13 Flight Journal - Day 3, Part 2: 'Houston, We've Had a Problem'," NASA (NASA), accessed May 23, 2020, https://history.nasa.gov/afj/ap13fj/08day3-problem.html.
- [10]Greg Holder. "God Help Us: Be Filled With The Spirit." (sermon, The Crossing Church, Chesterfield, MO, February 23, 2020).
- [11]*Cinderella*, DVD, directed by Kenneth Branagh (Burbank, CA: Walt Disney Pictures, 2015).
- [12]Hoda Kotb and Jane Lorenzini, *I Really Needed This Today: Words to Live By* (New York: G.P. Putnam's Sons, an imprint of Penguin Random House LLC, 2019), 104.
- [13]Angela Thomas et al., *Revitalize Your Spiritual Life: a Woman's Guide for Vibrant Christian Living* (Nashville: Thomas Nelson, 2010), 183.
- [14]"The Wheel Illustration," The Navigators, accessed May 23, 2020, https://www.navigators.org/resource/the-wheel-illustration/.

Chapter Seven:

- [1]Thomas J. Wurtz, *Corporate Common Sense: Revolutionary Business Lessons Inspired by Thomas Paine* (Bloomington, IN: AuthorHouse, 2009), 256.
- [2]Matt Chandler, Josh Patterson, and Eric Geiger, *Creature of the Word: the Jesus-Centered Church* (Nashville, TN: B & H, 2012), 176.
- [3]Simon Sinek, *Start with Why: How Great Leaders Inspire Everyone to Take Action* (London: Portfolio/Penguin, 2011), 7.
- [4]John C. Maxwell, *The Complete 101 Collection* (Nashville, TN: Thomas Nelson, 2012), 199.
- [5]Rick Warren (@RickWarren). 2014, "The First Job of Leadership Is to Love People. Leadership

without Love Is Manipulation.," Twitter October 22, 2014, 11:18 a.m. https://twitter.com/ RickWarren/status/524942786152652801.

- [6]"Learning by Teaching Others Is Extremely Effective – a New Study Tested a Key Reason Why," Research Digest, May 4, 2018, https:// digest.bps.org.uk/2018/05/04/learning-by- teaching-others-is-extremely-effective-a-new-study- tested-a-key-reason-why/.
- [7]Michael Bungay Stanier, *The Coaching Habit* (Toronto, Ontario, Canada: Box of Crayons Press, 2016), 60.
- [8]Jennifer Lee, *The Book Of Quotes*. (Queensland, Australia: Essentially Organized, 2020), 25 "The Book Of Quotes," Google Books (Google), accessed May 23, 2020, https://www.google.com/ books/edition/The_Book_Of_Quotes/ _13aDwAAQBAJ?hl=en.
- [9]John MacBeath and Neil Dempster, *Connecting Leadership and Learning: Principles for Practice* (N.p.: Taylor & Francis, 2008), 32 "Connecting Leadership and Learning," Google Books (Google), accessed May 23, 2020, https://www. google.com/books/edition/ Connecting_Leadership_and_Learning/ mNJ9AgAAQBAJ?hl=en.
- [10]Roger Gill, *Theory and Practice of Leadership* (London, UK: Sage Publications, 2006), 252.

Chapter Eight:

- [1]"USNWC Alumni," USNWC Alumni - "Leadership is building a bridge that..., accessed May 23, 2020, https://www.facebook.com/ USNWCAlumni/photos/leadership-is-building-a-bridge-that-connects-the-vision-with-the-purpose-in-ord/336655450379355/.

- [2]Santiago Jaramillo, "Council Post: Four Lessons From Companies That Get Employee Engagement Right," Forbes (Forbes Magazine, June 22, 2018), https://www.forbes.com/sites/forbeshumanresourcescouncil/2018/06/22/four-lessons-from-companies-that-get-employee-engagement-right/.
- [3]John Coleman and Kristi Hedges, "To Find Meaning in Your Work, Change How You Think About It," Harvard Business Review, February 4, 2020, https://hbr.org/2017/12/to-find-meaning-in-your-work-change-how-you-think-about-it.
- [4]"Vision," Dictionary.com (Dictionary.com), accessed May 23, 2020, https://www.dictionary.com/browse/vision.
- [5]William Wan, "The Coronavirus Pandemic Is Pushing America into a Mental Health Crisis," The Washington Post (WP Company, May 4, 2020), https://www.washingtonpost.com/health/2020/05/04/mental-health-coronavirus/.
- [6]Emmy Betz et al., "Covid-19 and Suicide: an Uncertain Connection," STAT, April 21, 2020, https://www.statnews.com/2020/04/22/suicide-covid-19-uncertain-connection/.
- [7]Fred Hutto, *The Pattern* (N.p.: Xulon Press, 2011), 30.
- [8]"Watch: Jesus Film Project," Watch | Jesus Film Project, accessed May 23, 2020, https://www.jesusfilm.org/watch.html.
- [9]Francis Chan and Mark Beuving, *Multiply: Disciples Making Disciples* (CO Springs, CO: David C Cook, 2012), 52.
- [10]Jack Adler, *Soulmates from the Pages of History from*

Mythical to Contemporary, 75 Examples of the Power of Friendship (New York: Algora Pub., 2013), 193.

- [11]"G652 - Apostolos - Strong's Greek Lexicon (KJV)," Blue Letter Bible, accessed May 23, 2020, https://www.blueletterbible.org/lang/lexicon/lexicon.cfm?Strongs=G652.
- [12]"G4129 - Plēthynō - Strong's Greek Lexicon (KJV)," Blue Letter Bible, accessed May 23, 2020, https://www.blueletterbible.org/lang/lexicon/lexicon.cfm?Strongs=G4129.
- [13]"Current World Population," Worldometer, accessed May 23, 2020, https://www.worldometers.info/world-population/.

Made in the USA
Monee, IL
19 August 2020